RANCH HOUSE
STYLE

RANCH HO

USE STYLE

KATHERINE ANN SAMON   PHOTOGRAPHS BY EDMUND BARR

Clarkson Potter/Publishers

New York

FOR MY PARENTS,

PEGGY AND JAMES,

WHO BUILT THEIR RANCH HOUSE IN 1964

Published by Clarkson Potter/Publishers,
New York, New York
Member of the Crown Publishing Group,
a division of Random House, Inc.
www.randomhouse.com

CLARKSON N. POTTER is a trademark and
POTTER and colophon are registered trademarks
of Random House, Inc.

Printed in China

Design by Jan Derevjanik

Library of Congress Cataloging-in-Publication Data
Samon, Katherine Ann.
    Ranch house style/Katherine Ann Samon;
    photographs by Edmund Barr.
    Includes bibliographical references and index.
    1. Ranch houses—United States. I. Title.
    NA7205 .S26 2003
    728'.373—dc21   2002073760

ISBN 0-609-60628-X

10 9 8 7 6 5 4 3 2 1

First Edition

CONTENTS

the new cool ranch

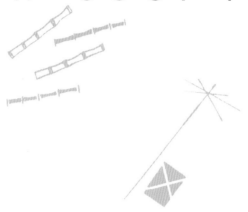

The modern ranch house was created as a gift for a specific audience: the new American family. But despite contributions from some of America's top-tier twentieth-century architects—such as Frank Lloyd Wright, Charles Eames, and William Wilson Wurster—the ranch fell out of favor for a while. Now the ranch is chic again, prized by new generations who value the style as much for its nostalgic appeal as for its graciousness and easy livability. The ranch's confident lack of pretension is finding renewed appreciation, and its star is in ascension.

That so many talented architects in the thirties and forties devoted themselves to this house form, and addressed such an intimate audience as the family, is extraordinary. Consequently, the house exists in both traditional and modern forms, in execution from high-brow to low. By the fifties and sixties, the ranch house—in all its regional adaptations—dominated the American landscape. It was the American Dream House.

One-story living provided convenience for raising children and enfolding older family members, and also estab-

lished the house's connection with the land—the ability to move outdoors from any room, to incorporate the outdoors into daily lives. It had a structural openness that came from tall ceilings and rooms that flowed into one another. The ranch pioneered the open plan between kitchen and family room that grew into the great room that was so popular in the eighties.

The early ranch houses, with their understated façades, were cherished by that era's Hollywood elite. Indeed, the image of the ideal American of the time could easily be summed up with the film persona of Gary Cooper—who lived in a ranch house. As director Frank Capra once expressed, "That guy just represents America for me." Like Cooper, the ranch extolled many of the same ideals of the forties and early fifties: of the modest and highly capable individual, devoted to family, with a directness and a lack of boastfulness that were powerfully engaging. These same elements are part and parcel of the ranch.

The ranch is the only house style I have ever lived in. I grew up in my parents' 1964 ranch house, in the same sub-

The exuberance of mid-century design is found in the car-obsessed influence of vinyl upholstery and chrome chair arms; in the sheer fun of a "marshmallow" floor lamp; and in the space-age sputnik ceiling fixture.

division of ranches that included my grandmother's house, built in 1956, and my aunt's house, built in the late sixties, all within an easy walk of one another. Even when I lived in New York City high-rises, my summer rental in the Hamptons was a ranch. And when it was time for my husband, son, and me to move to the suburbs, it was to a ranch house. This is the book I wish I'd had at my side when we moved into our house.

Past or present, owners of ranch houses have never had the same temperament as buyers of traditional two-story styles. The ranch is thoroughly modern: freer, with rooms that flow; less conspicuous, blending more with the horizon and its natural surroundings; more intimate, devoted to the quality of the lives inside it, not putting primary concern on curbside impressions. And this modern sensibility also affords a valuable freedom: to renovate or remodel, to add on or strip down. Restoring or adding elements of the great ranch houses of the past is the foremost desire of today's owners, who want to update (and often expand) their houses while maintaining one-story living. The ranch's

form readily responds to a range of possibilities: French doors can be added to the master bedroom to open onto a patio, or added to a breakfast room for integration with a garden; ceilings can be raised; outdoor spaces such as courtyards can be introduced. The potential for alteration is limitless; the wise buyer should view the existing structure as a starting point.

Not all ranches are vintage period pieces requiring restoration: unlike other American styles such as the bungalow that spoke specifically to the family, the ranch is the only one that has continued to proliferate. It endures because its fluid architecture enables it to easily adapt to the latest needs and expectations of contemporary lives. Its open, rambling quality and the generously sized plot that accompanies it evoke a spirited, western love of land, while its straightforward architecture projects solidness and dependability. It endures because it has the all-American combination of being both practical and romantic, both productive and generous.

At its beginning, the ranch was about innovation, exuberance, and accomplishment, fueled with extraordinary hopefulness. It was about informality and family. And on some levels, in the fifties, it was also simply about fun. All of these elements still combine to make the ranch house resonate with Americans across the country, again having a resounding and liberating impact on our lives.

Ranch Revival

The houses chosen for this book illustrate how the best of ranch-house living can be attained, in a range of styles and sizes and a range of renovation. The ways in which Americans approach ranch houses today are clear reflections of how our tastes and needs have evolved. We prefer even more openness in our rooms and in the flow from one area to the next. We long for light. We want additions for homes that might have been satisfactory in the past but now seem too small. A stronger indoor-outdoor relationship is high on lists. We dream of complete renovations or building from scratch as ways of demonstrating all our desires. As for style alone, we aspire to décor that is as chic as it is livable.

Most important, running through all these homes, old or new, traditional or modern, is one thread: the commitment to classic one-story living. Consequently, the most rewarding changes in all of the homes are in many ways restorations—bringing back the details that made ranch houses architectural gems when they first came on the scene, and continue to make them practical and sophisticated responses to the way we live today. All of these wishes, from basic to sweeping, are realized on the following pages, in the following categories:

Adding On

Many of the ranches built in the forties and fifties were modest two- or three-bedroom homes. Particularly in the forties, they were developed in response to a housing shortage for the middle class and were kept on the smaller side by high construction costs.

New owners are redrawing those basic shoebox shapes to create larger footprints, often with extra wings. Usually the additional space goes toward larger kitchens, creating master suites, or adding a family room or extra bedrooms. And these days, expansions are frequently focused on unusual enterprises, such as the formation of elegant, one-of-a-kind outdoor spaces.

Early History Lessons

For the first indications of ranches, most historians look to the early- to mid-nineteenth-century Hispanic ranchos and to their Anglo adaptations starting around 1850. From about 1905 through the mid-1920s, the bungalow influenced future ranches with their single-story low-pitched roof and emphasis on informal life. At around the same period, Prairie house architects opened up interiors and emphasized low horizontal exterior lines. Their influence was seen in the thirties when Frank Lloyd Wright created his landmark Usonian houses and when architects across the country began designing ranch-style houses. Technology joined in, with the creation of assembled materials. After World War II, the ranch's evolution progressed even more swiftly, with subdivisions built by everyone from high- to low-end architects, builders, and contractors, and ranches were rapidly on their way to becoming the most-built house type in America's history. In this chapter, a working ranch, an industrial designer's dream, and a fifties tract house take three stages of the history full circle.

Style Changes

The excitement that new owners of ranch houses feel when they're buying a home that appears to have little character, or seems frozen in time, comes from their ability to see that the limitations are merely cosmetic. This practiced eye goes past the below-average showing that some ranches might project and makes a perceptive face light up with the knowledge that a focused approach for interior and exterior can completely turn a house around. Style changes alone—without moving even one wall—can create a home that's not only sophisticated but highly original.

Moving Walls and Medium-Level Renovations

Often, style improvements alone are not sufficient. This dilemma arises when owners feel that even with cosmetic improvements, their house remains too dark, that rooms are small and closed off, and that the flow is cramped or awkward. Yet they are not prepared for the commitment of a full renovation.

The compromise is to rewrite the floor plan by moving—or removing—walls. Opening up a room, or combining two, brings in light and frees up circulation. Kitchens, living areas, and master bedrooms are usually the focus. With opened or enlarged rooms, spaces become better connected, the flow is easier, and the feeling in the home is more relaxed, expansive, and comfortable.

The next step, a medium-level renovation, should not only satisfy the personal wishes of the current owners but also give a house long-term appeal. In renovations of this scale, kitchens are frequently overhauled, and the home's floor plan is often amended to create better flow and to shape more-ideal rooms. Ceilings are raised and expanses of glass are inserted for more air and light.

At this level of change, the ranch house comes close to being rewritten, not only with a new look but with a higher level of functioning.

Complete Renovations and Newly Built

In this complete renovation, the owners held on to the footprint of the house, finding the amount of space satisfactory. Most of the house was gutted, redesigned, and totally updated, transformed into a ranch that became new again.

In three other situations, when opportunities arose to build their houses, these owners were unshakable in their belief that their homes should be ranches in every aspect, going against the grain of Tara-esque fantasies, faux estate-mansions, or characterless contemporary-traditional styles. Instead, they wanted the ease of one-story living, the pleasure of stepping outdoors from almost every room, of being connected to their land rather than plopped on it or towering over it. And most of all, they sought a practical home that would support their day-to-day living. Building their dream houses was not the culmination of dreams, it was the beginning.

In an eloquent blend of past of present, Lake/Flato architects combine modern design with familiar frontier forms.

ranch history

From the image of a cowboy hitching his horse to a frontier ranch to a fifties family piling into a station wagon in a suburban driveway, the ranch house evokes the evolution of a friendly, casual, and gracious house. "It's comfort architecture," says Terence Riley, chief curator of architecture and design at the Museum of Modern Art in New York City, of a house style made only in America. In the South and West, the suburban classic is called a "ranch-style house," because "ranch house" implies that the house is on an actual ranch. In other parts of the country, it's simply a "ranch." And for academics, it's a house *type*, not a style. But they all point to a one-story structure with strong horizontal emphasis, seeming to hug the ground, with larger ranches giving the impression of rambling over their terrain; the house usually has a low-pitch roof and overhanging eaves, and it is often in a rectangular or L shape with a cross-gable that breaks up the horizontal roof line.

At the time when ranch-style houses were created, in the late 1920s and the 1930s, they were considered a radical new way of living, with their open plans and the omission of formal rooms, and often the elimination of some interior walls. Their unassuming front façades, while attractive, were a puzzle, projecting no social or financial ranking. The design liberated the way Americans thought about houses—and the way they lived in them. Even the most stellar ranch appeared unconcerned with status.

Instead, the goal was to connect the people within and to induce them to lead expansive, open-minded lives. With low-key front façades providing privacy from the street, the house opened up completely in back—a radical move, creating a new way of living, inside and outside, by eliminating the division between the two spaces. "The principle concern in the design of the ranch house was with the quality and nature of lives. The ranch was an invitation to live intertwined with one's family and with the out of doors," says Kevin S. Alter, Sid W. Richardson Centennial Professor of Architecture and associate dean of architecture at the University of Texas at Austin.

The ease of informal ranch living is what makes this architectural style endure, along with a spirit-soothing

Previous page: The Herbert Jacobs House, built in 1936 in Madison, Wisconsin, was the first of Frank Lloyd Wright's Usonian houses. (Photograph by Paul Rocheleau)

sense that it is part of the American land, rather than towering over its site or being plopped onto it. It is a form that was created in the United States, specifically for the American family. And, typical of its open-minded mission, it continues to develop.

Early History: Spain, Mexico, and the Working Ranch

The earliest Hispanic contributions to the ranch house as it is known today are traced to the 1820s in the West, around the time that Mexico gained its independence from Spain (1821). "The houses that influenced later designers were the ones built by the Spanish and Mexican elite, mostly in the 1830s, '40s, and '50s," says Mark L. Brack, Ph.D., a scholar of early-California architecture and professor of architecture at Drexel University in Pennsylvania. "And very few of those survive."

Grand ranchos appeared on the scene at that time because of the secularization of great areas of mission land, intended to be returned to the Native Americans but ending up primarily in the hands of well-placed Mexicans. "The value of these lands included cattle, agricultural systems, and aquaducts," notes Brack. One surviving adobe hacienda from 1834 is Casa Grande, outside Petaluma, California, built for General Mariano Guadalupe Vallejo on a 44,000-acre ranch.

Made of adobe, the elite houses of this period tended to be low and spreading, in an L or U shape, sometimes even two-story. They had an outside *portale* or *corredor,* a covered porch that wrapped around the outside of the structure or around an interior courtyard. "The *portale* was their access from one room to another—there was no interior hall," Brack explains. "It was tradition in the Hispanic domestic arrangement to have extended families in the house and to have single rooms, so this setup also allowed privacy." It also afforded protection from sun and rain and provided a gathering place. Roofs were made out of reeds or, more scarcely, tiles. Floors were packed dirt or sometimes brick. Holding up the adobe walls were foundations made from stones, giving the impression that the houses grew out of the ground. It is to these Hispanic houses that twentieth-century architects turned in their interpretations.

The second wave of colonial influence came from the East, as new immigrants headed west to California in the 1820s. "The first large sawmills in the West were started by Anglos, often with the capital gained by marrying into the families of prominent Hispanic ranchos," says Brack. Sawmills allowed the large-scale production of roofs, shingles, wood frames, posts, doors, and window frames.

After the California Gold Rush of 1849, which brought such a population influx that California was admitted to the Union as a state in 1850, a new style of architecture appeared and proliferated, becoming a standard by the 1860s: board-and-batten houses. These are made from wide boards that were vertically laid, with a narrow piece of board (the batten) then laid over the seams. "It was a common building technique on ranches," Brack observes, "used for everything from sheds to barns and houses." These houses mimicked the low-lying quality of the Hispanic ranchos, and borrowed the one-room-deep layout, including the *portale*. Because board-and-batten structures were inexpensive, simple to build, and practical, they became typical of working ranches in the West and Southwest. For many of the same reasons, board-and-batten found its place in twentieth-century modernism.

Prairie Style and Bungalows

In Chicago suburbs at the turn of the twentieth century, a new house form emerged. The Prairie Style offered a fresh alternative to prevailing trends of jumbled roofs, cut-up interiors, and small windows. Frank Lloyd Wright (1867–1959) emerged as its leader. "Up until that time, houses were English Tudor, French Provincial, or Cape Cod Colonial—all derivative of styles from Europe, with Victorian houses being a mishmash of everything," says

Bruce Brooks Pfeiffer, director of the archives at the Frank Lloyd Wright Foundation in Scottsdale, Arizona, and coauthor of *Frank Lloyd Wright: The Masterworks.* "Wright believed in a future of developing an architecture that was integral to and belonged to the American soil. He was trying to give America an American home."

Echoing the flat planes of the prairie, the houses were compatible with their environment. Although they were mostly two-story, they seemed lower to the ground because of a gently sloping rather than steep roof. The roof projected over second-story windows to provide shelter for bands of casement windows and to emphasize horizontal lines. Extended terraces for second-floor rooms, and generous use of French doors, connected the houses to the outdoors. "Associating more with the garden and the landscape is the core of a Prairie house," notes Pfeiffer.

The houses were significant in another way: Wright went on record saying that he was developing a house that was less of a box, inside and out. For interiors, he created a more open plan, allowing rooms to flow together by eliminating unnecessary walls and doors. Pattern books published in the Midwest for the Prairie houses made it possible for the style to spread to suburbs across the country, until its decline after World War I.

Aspects of the bungalow would also find their way into ranch houses. "Today, people tend to use the term *bungalow* to refer to the Craftsman style," says Virginia McAlester, coauthor with Lee McAlester of *A Field Guide to American Houses,* "but in the bungalow era starting at the beginning of the 1900s to 1925 and 1930, the word *bungalow* was used for almost any one-story house." While always projecting a spacious, covered front porch, bunga-

lows came in a variety of styles, such as Spanish bungalows with red-tile roofs and wrought-iron fixtures, and Tudor styles displaying high-pitch gable roofs and prominent chimneys. "The most popular was always the Craftsman, or California bungalow, as it was called during that era, which almost always had a low-pitched roof," says McAlester. The bungalow's low roofline and the era's preference for one-story living became hallmarks of ranch houses.

"A large number of pattern books appeared, and this kind of one-story house received significant publicity in popular magazines such as *The Architect, House Beautiful* and *Ladies' Home Journal*," says McAlester. In the East, Gustav Stickley was building his Craftsman houses and, influenced by a visit to California, began designing bungalows, offering free plans in his magazine *The Craftsman*—which no doubt reinforced the national use of the term Craftsman Bungalow. Built through the mid-twenties, bungalows were the most popular house type for middle-class families.

Like the ranch, the bungalow was built for America's families, and its rise in popularity was fueled by the same two industries. "Financing for the middle-class home owner was made available for the first time," says McAlester, "with long-term installment-payment mortgages rather than having to pay cash up front or in a very short span." Decades later, the ranch would receive the benefit of long-term, government-sponsored loans. But the bungalow's longevity, unlike that of its successor, was cut short by the Depression. The second impact was transportation. "Entire neighborhoods of bungalows were built around electric trolley stops," says McAlester. Walking home was made easy because the narrow dimension of the bungalow faced the street and the long dimension was parallel to the side lot lines, allowing houses to be quickly passed by foot.

The bungalow's low lines and single floor had long-reaching impact. Exposed roof beams are one characteristic of the Craftsman bungalow. (Courtesy of the Archives at the Pasadena Historical Museum)

In contrast, people reached ranch house subdivisions by automobile. "Automobiles allowed the long dimension of the house to spread along the street, which was a luxury of land use that was not practical in the pre-automobile era," says McAlester.

The bungalow's interior world held its own significance. "Bungalows promoted informal family life," says Stephen Fox, an architectural historian, a fellow of the Anchorage Foundation of Texas, and a lecturer at Rice University and the University of Houston. "The idea was to open up the house. So instead of wasted hallway space such as a foyer, now you would enter directly into the living room, which opened directly onto the dining room. Bookshelves with pillars might separate rooms, but you would not see a wall with a door."

Because of the structure of these houses, says Fox, "Bungalows gave the ranch its informality, its openness, and its attunement to family."

Regionalism

For the wealthy in the 1920s, the trend had been to historical European styles of architecture, and also to mansions with effusive, picturesque historicism. The Great Depression brought a halt to this trend. An appreciation for simpler, indigenous buildings was growing, helped by the Historic American Building Survey, a 1930s make-work project for architects and draftsmen that required them to create drawings of historic buildings throughout the country. "It brought them in firsthand contact with significant historic buildings in whatever part of the country they happened to be working in," Stephen Fox explains, "and often made architects aware for the first time of their own local building traditions." Vernacular buildings (simple homes, farms, and ranches) gained a new respect that would show up in the design, construction, and invention of modern ranch houses. The Historic American Building Survey presaged the turning inward, away from Europe and toward a new American-born style of architecture and design that helped shape American modernism.

Frank Lloyd Wright and Usonia

The Depression caused rethinking even in the highest echelons of architecture. In the thirties, Frank Lloyd Wright developed his Usonian homes (*Usonia* was an acronym for the United States of America). "Wright wanted to provide

a beautiful home for a family of moderate income," says Bruce Pfeiffer. "His Usonian homes were different from anything else being built in the nation at that time." They were in direct contrast to traditional, formal, symmetric houses that had columns, pediments, and dark, boxlike rooms.

The first Usonian house was built in 1936 for Herbert Jacobs, in Madison, Wisconsin, and can be considered, according to Pfeiffer, "the true prototype of the Usonian house built over the next twenty years." The one-story, flat-roof house was designed in an L shape, allowing it to be positioned in a corner of the lot so that its back opened to the maximum expanse of green, and allowing the living and sleeping areas to open onto the terrain through French doors. While the front was almost windowless except for clerestory windows, the back was completely open, with full-length walls of glass and glass doors. The brick-and-wood Jacobs house was built for $5,000, and Wright's fee was $500.

"After the Depression, Wright believed that the plan of

In 1902, Frank Lloyd Wright built this Prairie Style house for Ward W. Willits of Highland Park, Illinois. (Photograph by Paul Rocheleau)

a home should be simpler," Pfeiffer explains. Wright omitted the parlor and the reception room, permitting the living space to be entered directly. He gave the house separate zones for living, with the living room on one side, bedrooms on the other, and the dining room and kitchen in between. "He felt that the kitchen should be an alcove off the dining and living area, so that the housewife was not sequestered but was a part of the activity of the family," Pfeiffer continues. As in his Prairie homes, Wright's interiors had an open plan, eliminating walls and doors whenever possible and allowing rooms to flow into one another.

Also echoing his Prairie homes are the strong horizontal lines of the Usonian houses. As in the Jacobs house, the beauty of the exterior comes from an unpretentious presentation of horizontal lines, and with a seamless blending with its terrain, realizing Wright's "organic" architecture whereby a house "grows easily from its site."

Through 1954, Wright built fifty-eight Usonian houses in nineteen states: Alabama, California, Connecticut, Illinois, Indiana, Iowa, Maryland, Massachusetts, Michigan, Missouri, New Hampshire, New Jersey, New York, Ohio, Pennsylvania, South Carolina, Virginia, Wisconsin, and Wyoming. Although the houses varied by client (one key option being roofs that were pitched, hipped, or flat), Wright developed a building system that included masonry walls for support; heating coils beneath the concrete slab for heating; a small below-ground space rather than a basement for a furnace; and carports instead of garages. In his Usonian houses, Wright built privacy and freedom of movement into houses for the middle class, and created the house form that had a resounding impact on architecture. In many ways, he created the model for all significant modern ranch-house architecture that followed—all of whose architects were great admirers of Wright.

Ranch House Architects

"While the way the modern ranch house functions is important," says Clifford Clark, author of *The American Family Home, 1800–1960* and Hulings Professor of American Studies at Carleton College in North Field, Minnesota, "the image that the house projects—easygoing, informal, healthy, and outdoors-oriented—is equally impor-

Sunset magazine, a champion of ranch houses, featured the Gregory Farmhouse, designed by William Wilson Wurster, in the center of one of its covers. (Courtesy of Sunset Publishing Corporation)

tant. And in California in the 1920s and 1930s, Hollywood and southern California promoters created that easy, Mediterranean, outdoors lifestyle." The citrus industry, the railroad, and the movie industry were instrumental, as was *Sunset* magazine.

Sunset was started in 1898 by the Southern Pacific Railroad as a travel magazine to lure people west. In 1928 it was bought by Laurence Lane and transformed into a lifestyle magazine. "From the beginning, it was a regional magazine, celebrating the western difference—that ability to live indoors and outdoors all year," says Daniel Gregory, Ph.D., an architectural historian and a home editor at *Sunset* magazine in Menlo Park, California. The magazine had been looking for architects and designers who had a story to tell about the West and who were inventive. "And when they hit upon Cliff May in 1933, they kind of hit upon pay adobe, as we say," quips Gregory. Cliff May

(1908–1989), often called the father of the California ranch house, took a whimsical view of the elite Hispanic ranchos of the 1830s, '40s, and '50s and updated them. "He combined the romance of history with the pragmatism of the present, frequently filling his houses with inventions such as electric skylights," explains Gregory.

May, a former bandleader and furniture maker, began with speculative houses that he designed in an idealistic hacienda style. *Sunset* wrote, "May's house, stretching across suburban sites, rambled to almost the point of departure, with lines as natural and satisfying as those of the hills." Similarities to the ethos of Wright's Usonian houses are clear. "In fact, he was a great admirer of Frank Lloyd Wright," says Gregory. "May told me that he would occasionally fly down to visit Wright in Scottsdale. Other ways you see Wright's influence are in the open floor plan and the continuity between indoors and out, with houses that opened in back to landscapes or courtyards."

May's informal, affordable homes gave the impression of being very authentic, with rustic tile roofs, overhanging eaves, and complete with courtyards and patios that often featured fountains and wishing wells. Larger houses typically included stables in the plans. Inside, pitched ceilings had exposed rafters and heavy beams. Notes Gregory, "It was a romanticized version of the California dream that it helped market—a vision of California as the suburban Eden." In the late forties and fifties, May produced more purely modern homes full of the latest technology such as radiant floor heating and electric curtains.

May's success was helped by the home and women's magazines that lauded ranch living. He benefited by his *Sunset* association to such an extent that the only two books of national scope on suburban ranches are by *Sunset* with Cliff May in the forties and fifties. Even *Sunset's* offices in Menlo Park were designed by May, in 1950, opening in August 1951.

In addition to Wright's influence, May was also responding to the 1920s and 1930s work of William Wilson Wurster (1895–1973). A San Francisco architect, Wurster used early-nineteenth-century Monterrey structures as a jumping-off point for the development of his modern, regionalist idiom. Wurster became a dean at Massachusetts Institute of Technology in 1944, moving in 1950 to become dean of architecture at the University of

California at Berkeley through 1959. He then helped found and became dean (through 1963) of the College of Environmental Design, which incorporated the studies of architecture, city and regional planning, landscape architecture, and environmental planning. Wurster was also winner of a gold medal from the American Institute of Architecture in 1969.

Says Harrison Fraker, the current dean of the College of Environmental Design at the University of California, Berkeley, and a scholar of Wurster, "Wurster's aesthetic and intent are about a simple American life. His houses are understated in their direct, no-pretense approach. Wurster's planning takes into account the complete environment—climate, wind, and view. The power of his work can be felt in something as typical as a covered porch: At first, it seems like any porch. But sitting there, it's one of the most relaxed, comfortable, and serene experiences because it's been carefully planned."

One of Wurster's most famous works is the Gregory farmhouse, built in 1928 for Daniel Gregory's grandmother, and from which it's possible to see the influence on May's hacienda and board-and-batten houses. The Gregory farmhouse is essentially two L-shaped, informal houses, with a tall tower containing a bedroom, and with terraces and sleeping porches. Wurster made it out of vertical boards, without batten. Even so, says Mark Brack, "The mood is similar to that of the simple, mid- and late-1800s board-and-batten houses in California. That farmhouse helped set the tone for Wurster's suburban homes."

In response to the Depression, Wurster's early aim was to design smaller ranch houses that felt larger, drawing on elements of the Gregory farmhouse. "They are transitional houses in that they are reaching toward modernism in their open plan but traditional in their use of such details as double-hung windows and shutters," Gregory observes. "Wurster's houses were about simplification and functional form, minimizing decorative elements."

His ranch houses were informal and had an openness to the out-of-doors and a rambling nature. In fact, *Inside the Large Small House: The Residential Design Legacy of William W. Wurster* by R. Thomas Hille lays out the aspects of Wurster's houses that not only increased the feeling of space in a small house but that also are part and parcel of almost every ranch house: covered porches; terraces,

A home by Cliff May demonstrates his romanticized view of the hacienda. (From *Western Ranches* by Cliff May, courtesy of Hennessey + Ingalls)

decks, and gardens accessible through French or sliding doors; an emphasis on views and light achieved by using large windows and high ceilings; a maximization of space by incorporating multipurpose rooms, such as a kitchen–dining room combination; the use of inexpensive materials; clean, simple lines; and the omission of unnecessary details, such as molding, in order to draw the eye to the landscape. By the forties, his houses were more influenced by the International Style, becoming further abstracted.

Three other acclaimed architects were building ranch houses at the time, developing a regional response to the California ranch house and lifestyle: O'Neil Ford (1905–1982), a friend and protégé of Wurster's, working in Texas, translating local vernacular buildings into modern forms and materials; in the Pacific Northwest, Pietro Belluschi (1899–1994), taking over from Wurster as dean at MIT from 1951 to 1965 and a 1972 AIA gold medal winner, whose residential work incorporated local traditions and materials; and Harwell Hamilton Harris (1903–1990), in California, Texas, and North Carolina, who worked with Richard Neutra and whose use of wood often was evocative of Japanese structures.

While all of these architects responded to Wright's early work and to the open plan in his Usonian houses, they were all individually expressing the invention of the suburban ranch house. In almost a reverse commute, the news spread east across the country through architectural journals and popular magazines. The ranch house was at its professional height in the thirties and early forties, with the gems of these architects going to the American family.

Postwar America: The Forties

"In the forties, the nation underwent the largest surge of home construction since the twenties," says Clifford Clark of the postwar years. Euphoria about winning the war extended to a feeling that sacrifice was over, and there was a new dawn on many fronts. In the center of that new horizon would be the American dream house. "During the war years, because so much of the war effort was undisclosed, magazines focused a lot of attention on the postwar home. Fantasizing about how good life would be after the war, they looked, for example, to the home of the future, the kitchen of the future," explains Kevin Alter. "The ads would say, essentially, that the same technology that was winning the war would make the dream house fantastic when the war was over."

During the war, the Andersen Corporation offered a "Scrapbook for Your New Home" for collecting ideas for building a dream home. "By the war's end, Andersen had distributed over 350,000 copies," says Clark, demonstrating the pent-up desire for home ownership and family life.

When the war was over, millions of servicemen and

-women came home to face a housing shortage, and the country's war machines remobilized for housing. The Federal Housing Administration passed the GI Bill, providing government-guaranteed loans for returning servicemen to purchase, build, or improve houses, and thus making home ownership possible for the first time to a large percentage of the population.

"There was increased use of standardized materials and mass-production techniques, many of which had been learned in the war," Clark points out. "For instance, the creation of modular building products such as standardized sizes of Sheetrock and prefabricated window units. So now more people could afford houses, and they were cheaper and faster to build." With the economy expanding in the forties, the time was ripe for the building boom. Along with ranch houses derivative of the style of the thirties and early forties, entire developments of ranch houses were springing up.

In the last half of the forties, two very different sets of housing were under construction simultaneously, at opposite ends of the county.

On the East Coast, William Levitt was a pioneer of mass-produced housing. In 1946 he turned an area of Long Island, New York, into a fully designed community, with houses selling for $7,900 in either a ranch or Cape Cod style. The houses had radiant floor heating, picture windows, and expansion attics to allow the future addition of two more bedrooms, and they were offered with thirty-year mortgages with no down payment required for returning veterans. "Levitt sold more than 10,600 houses by 1950," says Clark. The eight-hundred-square-foot houses included a fireplace and appliances. For veterans used to renting or living with extended-family members, the houses were a boon.

"During the late forties, the construction cost of an average house doubled," says Clark. Most houses were small two-bedrooms that focused on practicality by incorporating multipurpose rooms such as the living-dining room.

On the opposite coast, in California, the Case Study project was under way. In 1945 John Entenza, the editor of *Arts & Architecture* magazine, commissioned architects such as Charles Eames, Eero Saarinen, Richard Neutra, Pierre Koenig, Craig Ellwood, and William Wilson Wurster to design new concepts of the open-plan house developed by Wright, with the only requirement being a comfortable living environment. The project began with the idea of modest cost, but it quickly soared. The wood- or steel-frame houses were built in the Los Angeles area, almost all of them one-story and constructed on flat slabs. Case Study houses appeared ultramodern in their purity of design, incorporating the International Style's influence of glass walls, flat roofs, and rectangular shapes. According to Esther McCoy, author of *Case Study Houses 1945–1962*, the groundwork for the houses had already been laid by the works of Los Angeles' concentration of talent such as Rudolph Michael Schindler, Gregory Ain, and Raphael S. Soriano. Their work, like the ensuing Case Studies, demonstrated "that a good house can be of cheap materials; outdoor spaces are as much a part of design as enclosed space; a dining room is less necessary than two

Left: Built by William Wilson Wurster in 1931 on a steep hill in Big Sur, California, the Voss house appeared to be simple upon approach. Right: In back, a full-length covered porch overlooked the ocean; underneath, large doors opened up the kitchen to a terrace. (Courtesy the Roger Sturtevant Collection, Oakland Museum of California; gift of the artist)

baths and large glass areas; a house should be turned away from the street toward a private garden at the back."

One of the most famous is 1959's Case Study #22, Pierre Koenig's 2,300-square-foot, L-shaped house designed on a pad at the edge of a precipice overlooking Los Angeles County. Steel decking is used for the street-side wall for privacy, while all of the other walls are entirely sheets of glass. In the crook of the L is the pool, set close to the cliff, allowing the water and sky to seem united. The house affords a 240-degree view of some one hundred miles and seems to merge with the sky and distant terrain. The last Case Study house, #28, was designed in 1966, in Thousand Oaks, by Buff, Hensman and Associates.

The Palm Springs Modern group has similarities to the Case Study houses: they were also primarily built from the mid-forties through the sixties, are mostly single story and flat roofed, and share some of the same architects, such as Richard Neutra, who was at the front of the Palm Springs group, and A. Quincy Jones. But the Palm Springs houses were usually much larger and sometimes carried a grander, more global statement about modernism.

Formerly, banks had been reluctant to offer construction loans or mortgages for modern houses, but the critical acclaim of the Case Study and Palm Springs Modern houses relaxed their policies, opening the door for more modern homes. The Case Study houses influenced suburbia across the country. "They have the same openness to the outdoors as the earlier great ranch houses, and the low spreading quality, though stripped of any historical detail," says Mark Brack. The war gave the Case Study architects new materials such as plastics, synthetic resins for weatherproofing, and aircraft glues for adhering laminates.

"The ranch house owes a debt to the Usonian houses and the Case Study houses," notes Alter. "They proposed new ways of living, liberating the house from the confines of tradition and habit." The ideas of independence and freedom that are built into the ranch had across-the-board appeal. "In terms of style, architects were freed from European historical models," explains Clark. "And on an individual level, the fact that you could have a house of your own was exciting. You could be independent."

A more casual lifestyle had firmly taken hold. "People were thrilled with newness and modernity," says Alter. "The house was literally opened and consequently the lives lived inside them were freed. The ranch was a hybrid of so many of the things that people liked: it had some tradition to it, but it was new and modern. It took popular aspects from a variety of traditions and was relatively unconcerned with decorum. In many ways, the ranch house liberated the way families lived."

The Fifties

The democratic ideal of the ranch house had great resonance. "Never before in history have so many people been able to afford their own home," says Terence Riley. "The sense of the individual is very strong in the modern era, and the ranch house is everyman's opportunity to express his individualism in architecture—a privilege that had not previously been accorded to the middle class. You might even say that the ranch created the middle class."

As much as it helped spawn a new kind of American family, the house responded to their needs. "The ranch house symbolizes the happy family, with no divisions between the areas for the master bedroom and the children's bedrooms," says Paul Groth, a vernacular architectural historian at the University of California at Berkeley. With the record births of the baby boom, the child-centric family embraced the ranch house as its popularity swept across the country, in harmony with the new relaxed view of parenting put forth by pediatrician Benjamin Spock, and the new idea that children could be fun.

The houses, influenced by the Usonian houses, had zones for living, with bedrooms for adults and children close together for the convenience of middle-of-the-night attention. In the center might be the kitchen, bathrooms, and utility room, for plumbing cohesion; farthest from the bedrooms were the living room and study. One-story living meant less separation. A new room off the kitchen, called the den, was geared to relaxing with the children.

The concept of the open kitchen—a radical idea—liberated the housewife by moving the kitchen from a far-off station to the center of the house and by removing walls that separated it so that it could flow into the den or living room or dining area. "As the kitchen is opened to the room where one entertains, for instance, the traditional role of the housewife has changed, and the social consequences of such a change are important—she has been to some degree liberated from the confines of simply service," points out Kevin Alter.

That liberated role helped empower the housewife. "In the fifties, the housewife received unprecedented emphasis," notes Stephen Fox. "She was the captain of the domestic ship." The new rambling houses required a central control point. "In some ranch houses, you find the kitchen in the front of the house, enabling the housewife to stand at the sink and see everyone who approaches. That's her surveillance post, and where she operates new machines and gadgets." Indeed, the housewife was the target of advertising and marketing not only for appliances but for everything necessary to fill a home.

Although it had a front door, the new ranch house was usually entered through the garage. Without a car, there could be no ranch house: the rise of the automobile allowed people to move farther out to cheaper land and therefore less expensive homes. Rambling, horizontal ranch houses were taking advantage of the larger plots—and quickened the constant shift from urban to suburban living. "Suburbia began with the expansion of our cities at the very beginning of the nineteenth century, first with walkable suburbs, then farther out with the steam ferry, the railroad, and the streetcar," says Alexander Garvin, professor of urban planning and management at Yale University, and author of *Parks, Recreation, and Open Space: A Twenty-First Century Agenda*. "The automobile is simply the second to last stage of suburban development; the newest suburbs are second homes in another state, accessible by airplane."

The interstate highway system had a dramatic effect on Americans. "It was begun during the war to accommodate munition factories that were dispersed throughout the country, and allowed wartime towns to be quickly built," Alter explains. "In the fifties, those highways allowed the public unprecedented access to the country." The West Coast buildup for the military was particularly extraordinary. "From 1941 to 1945, 500,000 people moved to Los Angeles alone. People were moving across state lines in record numbers." The strong promotion of the sunny California lifestyle—its casual indoor-outdoor living; convertibles and highways; gardens, terraces, swimming pools, and backyard barbecues—was celebrated by journals and magazines.

A technological breakthrough that greatly benefited the ranch was air-conditioning. Units for the home had been developed in the thirties, but it was only after the war and the boom in housing that they became more compact and less costly. "Prior, in areas such as Houston, positioning bedrooms and living areas to receive cooling southeast breezes was very important and resulted in houses that were only one room deep," says Fox. "With air-conditioning, this was no longer a concern. Houses could be two rooms deep and positioned on a lot with concerns other than the prevailing breezes."

"Suburbia was welcome," notes Alter. "Children could play in the yard, not in a busy urban street. Your house was full of new and modern conveniences such as intercoms to communicate between rooms, percolators for coffee, televisions having a place of honor. In many ways the ranch house enabled a growing middle class to take pleasure in the modern world."

The ranch house was a kind of castle, its own world. "With the postwar focus on the family and the individual," Alter continues, "it stands to reason that the home would be conceived of as an enclave—you'd have these wonderful worlds inside of the ranch house that floated to the backyard with decks and patios and barbecues."

Gasoline was inexpensive, and so the car was as much a tireless toy as a means of transportation, becoming a significant part of the suburban landscape. Developers such as Joseph Eichler, who built modern houses in the San Francisco Bay area, sometimes designed carports in the front and center of the house.

"By the 1950s, people saw the garage as an important adjunct to the kitchen," says Groth. "Early on, the garage was largely a male domain. That's where men spent a lot of time washing their car and hanging out with their car, and it became, essentially, a substitute for the front porch. Almost immediately, women began to 'invade' the garage, often placing washer-dryers and spare freezers there."

Even glamorous ranch houses were part of this general milieu. "High-style ranch houses were really just like the fins on the 1958 Cadillac," observes Daniel Gregory. "They were long and low and expansive, and they symbolized the new racehorse in terms of housing. They represented modernity, and a place: the West." Just as some ranch house architecture was a romanticized view of the west, so were some of the era's televised Westerns. Settings for cowboys Gene Autry, Roy Rogers and Dale Evans, the Lone Ranger, and later the heroes of *Gunsmoke* and *Bonanza* were the television standards for decades.

In the mid-fifties, the Federal Housing Administration liberalized home loans and reduced down payments, and houses grew, says Clifford Clark. "By the sixties, two thirds of construction was for private houses, with the typical house size increasing from 800 to 1,240 square feet."

"The fifties were also a time of affluence and anxiety," continues Clark. "On one hand we were the most prosperous nation in the world, but the Cold War and atom bomb created a sense of anxiety." Many homeowners built backyard bomb shelters along with freestanding brick barbecues. "There was also the perfectionist impulse, everything from the perfect cake mix to the perfect house, and part of that desire for perfection is also a desire to control what is undesirable."

The suburbs grew at the expense of the cities, with the middle class realizing the dream of home-ownership, a decent plot of land, and a car in every driveway. One unfortunate result was the creation of new income-segregated neighborhoods, as former city dwellers established suburban enclaves that were, for the most part, almost entirely white. Intolerance rose, revealing the ugly side of some communities when homeowners fought against unwelcome arrivals. In 1954, the new suburbs were rattled by the Supreme Court's decision in *Brown* v. *Board of Education of Topeka* that separate education was not equal, and decreeing school desegregation.

Decline of the Ranch

While the ranch was the most popular style of housing through the sixties, there were rumblings. "People wanted a division of space," Clifford Clark explains. "They wanted a separate master suite, more closets." People who bought ranches in the fifties and sixties had often spent a period of time in married households with other adults. Because of the housing shortage and Depression, it was not unusual for grown family members to continue living together. So their acoustical experiences and privacy expectations had been modest, but increased with time and with the growth of their children. Consequently, the ranch house grew, typically incorporating four bedrooms, two and a half baths, a living room, kitchen and family room, utility room, study, and a two-car garage. As the kitchen and family room grew in size, they were usually more and more connected. "The one consistent feature in American home building in the postwar period is the consistent dramatic increase in the size of houses," notes Clark.

Teen culture transformed the ranch. "With an affluent society's discretionary income, teenagers' spending naturally encompassed music, causing the parents to build master suites upstairs to avoid the sound," says Clark. "A separate family room or playroom added more segregation in the house."

Teenagers felt that they had no privacy, nor did the suburbs provide interests for them the way that younger children's needs were met through parks. Housewives also felt isolated. Families were more scattered, often with both parents working and children going in separate directions in their own cars.

By the seventies, many earlier-built tract ranch houses were evincing the shortcuts taken during their construction: quickly and inexpensively built, they were breaking down, making the gloomy quality of low ceilings and dark rooms more obvious.

In a broader view, from the mid-fifties through the seventies, Americans experienced large-scale social and political movements, from Civil Rights to the rise of a drug and sex culture to women's rights and the Vietnam War. "I don't think that the decline of the ranch has anything to do with those social movements, but it was simultaneous to those events," says Alexander Garvin. "It was simultaneous to the beginnings of an urban revival, with young adults wanting the excitement and variety of opportunities available in cities that was not available in the suburbs." Suburbia and its ranch houses were regarded as conformist by some intellectuals, radicals, and nonconformists. As if to back up that impression, aerial views of young suburbs often showed uniformity. "But these particular circles of people were a very small percentage of Americans," says Garvin. "Most people were happily moving into their ranch houses and were happy to have a nice house in a nice neighborhood."

New construction showed changes in the seventies. To produce more affordable houses, "the building industry was increasingly removing any costly ornaments from the buildings," says Garvin. "The houses became simpler and simpler, causing dissatisfied consumers." The public did not react warmly to the stripped-down modernist versions of the ranch. "So you began to see what I call the 'heavy-handed Hispanic hacienda' and the 'columned Colonial cottage'—attempts to add ornamentation and to give people more than a box. Cathedral ceilings and patios were positive aspects of the trend, while other details, which were inexpensive and often overblown, also appeared, such as overdone porticos. "It's also in this period that houses begin to get larger and larger," says Garvin.

Starting in the eighties, the ranch encountered snob-

Houses in this new 1960 tract in Newbury Park, California, appealed directly to veterans. (Local History Collection, Thousand Oaks Library)

bery from the rise of urban, upwardly mobile young careerists who shunned middle-class associations. "Young professionals were striving to be more individual, yet often had a more traditional sense of elitism," Mark Brack explains. "Most of them came from middle-class backgrounds, and that's what they were trying to disassociate themselves from."

With empty lots growing scarce and expensive in prime locations, there was not enough land for sprawling homes. Consequently, the size of the house, often on smaller plots, became a primary concern.

In keeping with the desire for impression making, the eighties saw a dramatic shift to a seemingly opposite direction in the house orientation: vertically. "In the late eighties there was a move to having two-story spaces, such as tall foyers and great rooms," observes Paul Groth, "with the intention of giving a room more importance." The great room was a combination of kitchen, breakfast area, and family room, discernible as a further opening up of the ranch's layout.

The eighties and nineties were the era of the "McMansion." Garvin first heard the term in Atlanta around 1982. "McMansions are simply the larger, more expensive versions of the heavy-handed seventies houses," says Garvin. While always new construction, and always grand in presentation, a McMansion usually means a 5,000- to 10,000-square-foot two-story house, in stone or brick, often with columns and large car courts as well as three- or four-car garages. "A McMansion is not one house on its own, it's a subdivision of them, such as when one builder puts up eight of them on a cul-de-sac, and each of them is on a small plot of land."

John Milnes Baker, in *American House Styles,* notes styles such as the Builder's Contemporary, and Neo-Shingle, Neo-Classical Revival, Neo-Tudor, Neo-Mediterranean, Neo-French Eclectic, Nouveau-Traditional, and Neo-Victorian. The intent was an image that was the polar opposite of a ranch. However, according to Stephen Fox, "if you consider the rooms that they include and omit, and if you examine the ways the rooms are zoned, they are still a ranch, simply a bloated version." Subdivisions with names that included the word *Estates* sprang up, offering smaller versions—"Happy Meals"—that had busy, varied rooflines.

"In these starter mansions, one sees the physical embodiment of the desire for wealth and class. Principle among their characteristics was a change toward huge multifaceted roofs," says Alter, "which is clearly about showing off for the street."

Ranch Renaissance

To say that the ranch is returning is seemingly a contradiction. "The ranch has been continuously built since the thirties," says Paul Groth. Its revival at the start of a new century, however, is unmistakable.

With the houses passing their fifty-year mark, their place in American social and cultural history has increasing significance. Says Virginia McAlester, "Preservation should not be only of grand mansions but should very much encompass the way that the typical American family lived, and that is what the ranch house tells us so clearly. We see the ideals, lifestyles, and economy of one of the most important eras of American history."

For houses and neighborhoods to become eligible for the National Register of Historic Places, they generally must be at least fifty years old, and so, consequently, planning departments in cities are looking at ranch houses and ranch-house subdivisions from the 1940s and 1950s. "As ranch-house neighborhoods are being surveyed, they're positioned to be the next wave of historic districts, much as Tudor cottages from the twenties and thirties began being recognized in the nineties," says McAlester.

With a similar perspective, in 2002, the National Register of Historic Places, a program of the National Park Service in Washington, D.C., published an extensive work entitled "Guidelines for Evaluating and Documenting Historic Residential Suburbs for Listing in the National Register of Historic Places." Says Carol Shull, the Keeper of the National Register, "There is a growing interest in the pre- and post-WWII period and its significance in American architectural history. With the passage of time and with scholarship, the public begins to understand different property types as part of our heritage, and so there is recognition for the historic significance of forties and fifties architecture. In terms of impact, that was one of the biggest building booms, having profound effect on how people lived and worked."

Two ranch house suburbs that have been entered into the National Register are El Encanto Estates Residential Historic District in Tucson, Arizona, a district with a significant number of ranch houses, and Arapahoe Acres, in Englewood, Colorado, an area that demonstrates architect-developer collaboration. In Temple, Texas, the U-shape 1959 home of Ralph Wilson, Sr., the founder of Wilsonarts, has been given National Register status. The home was intended as a showcase for the company's production and multi-use of plastic laminate, commonly called Formica.

Increasing historical regard for homes such as ranch houses reflects a shift in American values. "We're living with less showing off and less irony," observes Kevin Alter, pointing to the current architectural revival. "People started to look again at what makes life pleasurable, and how architecture can help foster the central pleasures of life, and that makes ranch very appealing."

Within this mood, McMansions are experiencing a backlash. "The negative response comes from the sight of enormous houses shoehorned onto small sites," says Alexander Garvin, "as well as the message of conspicuous consumption." Preservation groups form to save ranches from being razed to make way for subdivisions of McMansions. "Every bit as important as an individual ranch house might be, the way in which they were grouped together and sited into unified street scapes is equally as important," says McAlester. "The interruption of those wonderfully calm, inviting, and uniform streets is one element of what people react to when they step in to save a home from being razed to make room for an oversize two-story home. It's one-story houses flowing into each other with the sudden break of an overly large two-story mass that is out of scale and that changes the scape."

Additional critics of overscale homes are beginning to be the owners themselves. Some inhabitants of trophy houses have diminishing desire for their homes as they find themselves dwarfed by the homes' exaggerated size. "The people with new wealth who used to seek out these houses now have a different perspective," says Clifford Clark. "They're looking toward understatement and refined craftsmanship as a means to define status." The Japanese component of ranch houses—their lack of affect, their melding into nature with simple materials, an honest presentation of construction, and a low, natural profile—has a sense of new discovery.

The fresh look at ranch houses is also due to a swing back and forth in architectural fashion. "Every generation always has a lack of appreciation for what was being built by their parents' generation," notes McAlester. "Thomas Jefferson railed against Georgian houses when he built Monticello in Early Classical Revival. It's a cycle we see, of generations treasuring the houses that their grandparents and great-grandparents lived in. And so Baby Boomers and subsequent generations are predictably appreciating ranch houses."

On a pragmatic level, the new perspective for ranch-house architecture is also due to the realities of the post-war generation's offspring. "As Baby Boomers become older, going up and down stairs becomes less attractive, making the one-story ease of ranch houses very appealing," says McAlester. Financially, from the building industry's point of view, a slower and more cautious economy means more restraint with building materials. To Garvin, the ranch house's value is that "it's easy and often less expensive to build, it's easy to maintain and live in, and it reflects a way of life that is very much American. We are an open and active kind of society."

The ranch's legacy is that it promoted informality, openness, a merging with the outdoors, and that it centered on family life. Part of that recognition contains a nostalgia component. Says Terence Riley, "It is familiar, almost familial architecture to a generation that grew up in them or grew up watching them on television."

In its rediscovery, the ranch is progressing to meet the needs of a new generation, as it historically has, embracing the pleasurable aspects of tradition and incorporating new opportunities of contemporary living.

An unselfconscious demonstration of American architecture, the ranch's message has resonated with Americans from the start. "One might easily expect that the ranch's domestic environment leads to an ease of personal expression, independence, and individuality," says Alter. "That open-mindedness, inventiveness, and easy willingness to evolve with the American family makes it a significant and distinctive part of our American landscape."

adding on

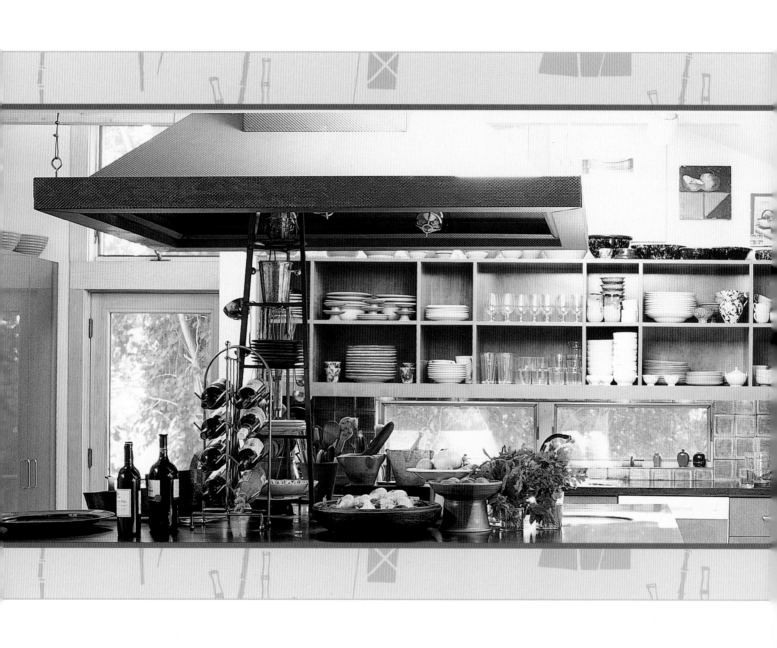

A COOK'S PARADISE

It's a perfect match. First, the quiet, untouched farm and wine country of the North Fork of Long Island, New York, where tractors are more common than Range Rovers and where the signs for roadside flower and vegetable stands are often painted by hand. And second, the owners of Frog Hollow Hall, two men whose idea of a brilliant weekend afternoon is not about shopping-to-be-seen or celebrity spotting, but about poking through farm stands for the freshest locally grown produce and plumpest homemade breads, then heading home to create a satisfying meal.

The addition is visible to the left of the entrance. To keep the mood of the home casual, a blue-green paint was selected.

Their 1979 house was a simple and small 850-square-foot ranch. Charles Morris Mount and Harold Gordon chose it because its three quarters of an acre, surrounded by untouched fields, leads down a slope to a large pond. "Because we loved the pond so much, we decided to call the whole place Frog Hollow Hall," says Gordon.

Mount, a New York interior designer with many restaurant clients, loves to cook. And both men prefer to socialize with friends and clients by hosting dinner parties rather than dining out. But this was barely possible in the house's cramped, closed-off kitchen, where a maximum of six sat knee to knee.

Inside the airy addition, half is the new kitchen pavilion and half is the new living room. The kitchen ceiling peaks at eighteen feet; the living room's, at twenty. But it is clearly the dramatically lit kitchen that is the crown jewel. "When you get right down to it, preparing dinner for people *is* a bit theatrical," Gordon admits. "It's like a performance. And these days, guests want to be a part of it."

So the practical, carefully laid-out kitchen also has generous space for guests to join in the preparation as well as gather around the island. "I love that I can cook and be among my guests instead of cut off in a separate room," says Mount. "Now it's a shared experience for everyone."

Previous page: The kitchen is filled with natural light from skylights, full glass doors, and a windowed backsplash, whose ribbed topaz tiles bounce light and add rich shimmer.

Ranch Style ENTRANCES

The artful presence of this house's front came about through problem solving. To the right of the front door (opposite) is a large bathroom window that needed to provide privacy and also to admit light. The owners installed a three-sided lattice screen that shields the window while filtering in light and adding texture and dimension. A planter built into the top of the screen secures cascading vines that suggest the gardening efforts in back of the house. The undrilled bowling balls are a sculptural, planetary play on the glass gazing balls often used as garden ornaments.

Ranch Style TEXTURES

In the addition, the chimney, corner piers, and low terrace columns repeat the materials of the living room's fireplace, with textures coming from bricks and split-face concrete blocks tinted a desert-sand color. The effect mimics expensive stone, creating a layered, patterned support structure that is carried into the interior.

From the back of the house: The façade fronting the twenty-foot-wide living room is meant to evoke nearby barns. Says Charles Mount, "The top window is like the hayloft, and the bottom glass doors are reminiscent of barn doors." Outside is a large raised terrace.

Ranch Style KITCHEN PLEASURES

The ranch house kitchen has always offered an abundance of pleasures and conveniences for cooking, from the first dishwashers in the 1950s to the more advanced accoutrements of today. Mount had the burners configured in a single row to avoid burns from reaching over a flame or pot; generous four-foot-wide paths lead around the island; a small island sink has a built-in rinsing colander; an open shelf of dish towels stands ready between stove and sink; ample electrical sockets are hidden on the underside of upper cabinets; and dimmers control every light in the kitchen, even those in the hood.

Right: An upper band of square windows delineates the kitchen pavilion. Powerful professional appliances are offset by the warmth of open maple upper cabinets. "Open cabinets are visually more exciting to me than closed doors," Mount explains.

Left: A generous six-by-eight-foot island has center-stage authority. The custom copper hood is suspended by steel cables over a professional grill and range top. The glass door in the kitchen leads to a deck (opposite, left).

Ranch Style **DINING AREAS**

The open dining area is a ranch-house hallmark. Here, the focus is the twelve-foot-tall custom ash bookshelf, most of which houses cookbooks. For the raised fir ceiling, custom plates, in black steel, act as anchors for the king-post trusses. Poised above the table, a custom copper-and-glass chandelier brings the eye downward to the table; it holds candles but also provides optional electric lighting. The Rais stove once heated the entire house and now has been refitted as a pizza oven.

Below: A deck off the kitchen offers privacy. Right: Even with its soaring ceilings, the dining room feels intimate.

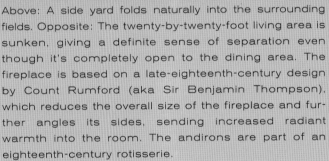

Below: "We often end up on the terrace after dinner to have dessert," says Mount. "You can see the reflection of the stars on the pond." The raised terrace is paved with the same blue stone as in the living room, in typical ranch-house style erasing the division between indoors and out. The deck chairs are from the 1920s.

Above: A side yard folds naturally into the surrounding fields. Opposite: The twenty-by-twenty-foot living area is sunken, giving a definite sense of separation even though it's completely open to the dining area. The fireplace is based on a late-eighteenth-century design by Count Rumford (aka Sir Benjamin Thompson), which reduces the overall size of the fireplace and further angles its sides, sending increased radiant warmth into the room. The andirons are part of an eighteenth-century rotisserie.

SECRET IN THE NEIGHBORHOOD

In this Austin, Texas, suburb full of ranches, it would be possible to car-pool right by this house and take it for granted, and the owners appreciate that. "It fits in very well with the neighborhood," says owner Chris Berry. But here and there is clear evidence that the owners think outside the box.

Chris and Celia Berry had been very specific about what they desired. "We have prejudice *toward* ranches," Chris acknowledges. "We think it's more important to live in an older, smaller house that feels good rather than a large one that's a bit generic." Celia, a mosaic artist, agrees from a design point of view:

"I love houses that are spread out into interesting shapes and are more in touch with the ground. I'm not a fan of two-story homes." And they actually wanted a house that needed updating. "We're both happiest when we have a project to work on," says Chris.

The area was once considered north of town, but it is now central to the city, with easy passage to downtown and Lake Austin and Lake Travis. Untouched since it was built in 1952, the house seemed ideal, with good structure and old trees on three quarters of an acre. But it was too small—at only eleven-hundred square feet, it needed to accommodate their young daughter, Madeline, two home offices, and frequent visitors.

So the rectangular two-bedroom was expanded with an L-shaped addition, forming a U. A new family room joins the original structure, with a master suite beyond. Matching the 1952-vintage exterior brick allowed a seamless transition to the addition. The new house is 2,050 square feet and creates a classic courtyard, inspired by the couple's love for Mexico. The new rooms and the renovated dining room all have glass doors that open onto the courtyard with its Canterra stone fountain.

Celia and Chris renovated and did the building themselves, which was doable thanks to the combination of Celia's creativity and Chris's abilities—a software engineer, he also has degrees in civil and structural engineering. They drew their own blueprints, got their own permits, and "did ninety percent of the work with friends," says Chris. They contracted out jobs such as tile, cement, and Sheetrock. "Although it took us two years, by doing it this way we could make the money go further. And we could concentrate on details to get a true hand-built quality."

The house thus became a gracious Mexican-influenced home, with the hallmarks of easy, natural flow and exuberant materials and colors. "It's the courtyard that makes the house unusual and so hospitable," Chris comments as he opens all the glass doors. "We can hear the fountain from practically every room in the house. The best thing is that because we installed it between our wing and our daughter's, at night we can all listen to the water from our bedrooms."

Previous page: The house's horizontal stretch gains grace from the sweep of mature trees and the gentle sidewalk curve.

"I prefer older homes for their character and the attention to detail," says Celia Berry of characteristics that are evident in the front façade.

Ranch Style VINTAGE

An uninhibited mix of detailing—celebrated rather than eradicated by the owners—is a hallmark of much 1950s design. On this porch, the treatments of those details give them new energy. The wood door is painted an electric indigo-violet. In contrast, the screen's overlay of metal bird and curlicue foliage—highlighting a mid-century love of motion—appear to be etched as a result of delicate pink paint. Geometric themes are seen in a lighthearted metal support that replays the rectangular cutouts on the door. Sidelights, repaired with matching rippled glass, carry through the theme and afford privacy and light. The bonnetlike metal awning is finished in the same cream as the house's trim.

Ranch Style **PORCHES**

The porch owes much of its vibrant mood to a careful use of color. Previously plain concrete, the porch was relaid with pink Canterra tile to make a soft, flowing transition from the sidewalk. A mosaic urn, made by Celia, anchors the space, lending artistry and a starting point for the Mexican-inspired theme indoors. Leading from the porch, flat sun-bleached stones fill paths through the yard, adding dimension. Party lights, chosen for their straight-forwardness, go off when the party ends.

Ranch Style **DOORS**

All of the doors and fixed-glass panels in the courtyard have uniform styling. "Rather than French doors, we wanted the more traditional look of separate, classic patio doors," says Celia. "In the family room, the center support that runs between the doors and up through the clerestory window gives that wall a feeling of strength." The doors admit full light and views, making the courtyard immediately present.

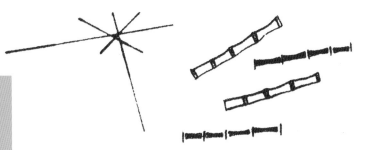

Opposite the fireplace, the family room opens onto the new courtyard. The clerestory window is exactly the same as the one over the fireplace, and it has the precise degree of curve as the pergola outside. "It brings light all the way through the room," says Chris of his design. The turquoise wash draws attention outward, and the expanse of glass allows even more light.

Above: For the new family room, friend and architect Tim Cross helped design the barrel-vaulted ceiling. "Done with wood, it's warm for a family room," Chris Berry notes. Here the wood is plybead (also called beadboard, it is plywood with vertical striations every one-and-a-half inches) with a natural stain. Below: To enhance a simple powder room, Celia was inspired by manuscripts and court paintings from India, designing her own stencils. To enlarge the usable space, the single door was replaced with a refined, space-saving set of two smaller ones.

The mosaic table, another of Celia's works, is where the family has almost every meal in good weather, and where every dinner party is invariably drawn.

Ranch Style COURTYARDS

An open arch, recurrent over many Mexican patios, gives the space a larger, more expansive feeling than a flat pergola would have. Chris and a friend welded the pieces themselves, then rested the structure on carved wood columns shipped from Oaxaca, Mexico. Plantings of wisteria, cross vine, star jasmine, and native grapes add fragrance and cover. The outdoor floor, like the porch, is pink Canterra tile. In original ranch style, the family traverses the patio to go from one room to another year-round. The classic tiered fountain comes from Mexico.

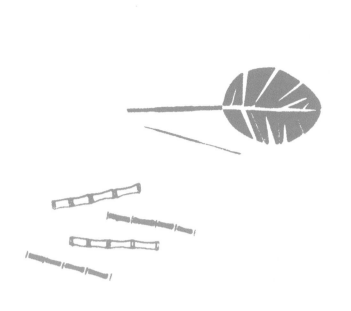

Celia rubbed yellow paint onto one wall of the dining room: "I thought it needed a vibrant color to accent the masks," she says of a collection from trips to Mexico, Africa, and Nepal. A hand-carved door from Mexico, leading to the family room, replaced a hollow-core door. The carved Indonesian bench is cushioned with fabric from India; chair seats are covered with Guatemalan textiles.

"The courtyard is our port against the storm," says Chris. "It reminds me of Mexico, where a family's courtyard is their privacy within the city."

Above: To keep the tones warm in the kitchen without detracting from the tile, butcher block was used on the stove surround. White floor tile replaced linoleum for an airy feeling. Behind the counter, a sunny wall of the dining room is now a natural extension of the kitchen.

Left: A colorful, sumptuous table is set with Mexican pottery, a harvest of peppers, and a statuette from Cairo (see no, hear no, speak no . . .).

Ranch Style
KITCHENS

The owners removed two walls of the kitchen, opening it to the rest of the house. The backsplash tile, seemingly Mexican in mood, "came with the house," Celia explains; on top, the couple built a counter with identical tile found locally. For dimension, she inserted a blue-rimmed tile pictorial, a memento of a trip to Portugal. They stripped and pickled the wood cabinets for a lighter effect and to save on expenses. The raised ceiling in the dining room defines and enlarges a separate area and expands the open feeling of the kitchen. Celia and Chris removed a small window and a door on the exterior wall, replacing them with a glass door centered between the two fixed-glass panels. This same three-piece glass system repeats in the master bedroom; a ranch house standby, glass walls eliminate indoor-outdoor division.

Ranch Style **BEDROOMS**

The warm-tone four-poster bed was a barter with Celia's brother-in-law; she gave him a handmade coat. "I wanted our bed to feel ornate and plush," she says. She beaded the embroidered side of the duvet, making it one-of-a-kind, and added a ruffle in tea-stained organza; the bed skirt is raw silk from China. Fabric from India was assembled for the center pillow, and the two large supporting pillows in back were sewn from fabric from Florence. Rather than a formal painting, a heavily beaded tapestry in similar tones is casually tacked behind the bed.

Even in the deliberately casual space, the bedroom offers richly detailed textiles. Celia beaded the duvet herself, and Chris brought the rugs home from Morocco.

"Lit from three sides, it's light all day," says Chris of the master bedroom addition, an effect enhanced by the ocher paint and vaulted tray ceiling.

ELVIS MEETS KUWAIT

It sits like a dare on the highest hill around, very, very sexy, and very strong. If it were a person, it would have its hands on its hips, defying time and place.

The flat roof suggests southern California's Case Study houses as much as it does the Palm Springs Modern movement and the Sarasota School of Architecture (Florida's modernist movement). But the house is located outside Austin, Texas, with commanding views of lakes, hills, and downtown.

Before its current splendor, it was orphaned for four years. Described as "International Style Ranch" on the real estate sheet, it had drawbacks beyond

Another hint of what lies inside: the miragelike view through the wall's door, all the way across the courtyard, to the front door, through the house, and on to a terrace door. Aluminum and glass doors replaced dark wood ones, polishing the modern mood.

that questionable characterization: the property was rimmed by a dark wooden fence resembling tall louvered shutters; it had only two bedrooms; and the inside color scheme, says owner Cindy Morgan, a graphic designer, "was classic eleganza—avocado and gold with brocade drapes everywhere." But what she and husband Clayton, a design consultant, recognized were some of the same qualities that international opera singer Willa Stewart desired when she built the house in 1972.

Two decades later, standing with their daughter and two sons, the Morgans were entranced instead of baffled by the house's interior arches and front pool. Its ten years of rough living as a rental could free them to think creatively rather than simply repair it, and living on one level seemed liberating. Taking in the quiet street in front and the diva views in back, they were convinced.

Previous page: The five-panel curve of glass is more like an outward pulse in the house's otherwise rectilinear geometry. The flat, bold roofline makes a strong, defining presence, while the perpendicular lines of the pool lead straight into the house.

The arches and flat roof held sway over Clayton. "It has aspects of the guest house on architect Philip Johnson's estate in New Canaan, Connecticut, which I love," he says. The Morgans' house does evoke many of the International Style's 1920s and 1930s hallmarks: generous use of glass, strong geometric shapes, asymmetry, and simple, unadorned lines. Additions to the house were made to reinforce that influence. Although the Morgans added two bedrooms for their sons, the more unusual enlargement was a private front courtyard that nearly doubles the living space. Clayton and Cindy enhanced the Mediterranean mood by bringing in twelve palm trees and building the tall, arched brick fence on two sides of the property for privacy.

The house has acquired a new drama, leading Clayton to call the sum total "Elvis Meets Kuwait." "Although today," he adds slyly, "he would be dressed in Prada."

Ranch Style
BUTTERFLY CHAIRS

Much furniture of this era folded for convenience, including the butterfly chairs beside the pool, derivative of Argentina's 1938 B.K.F. classic by Grupo Austral. The B.K.F. is also called the Butterfly, Sling, or Hardoy (after one of its designers), and is often associated with the 1950s and '60s. Although Knoll obtained the rights after the war, it lost a copyright suit because of the chair's diverse origins, beginning as an 1800s British Army camp chair, opening the way for imitators. Some estimates put the total number of chairs produced at about five million.

Ranch Style
COURTYARDS AND PAVILIONS

A classic L-shaped ranch helped create an enclosed courtyard: the front of the house forms one side of the courtyard, the bedroom wing forms another, and the two other sides are shaped by fences. Originally, this area had contained a small cement patio and patches of grass. The owners completely paved the space in limestone, which gives the illusion of white sand.

The outdoor pavilion—a popular feature of many ranches, for good reason—has the feeling of a true room, beginning with its careful placement along the length of the pool. The furnishings add sophistication and exotic notes. Flowing linen draperies provide the room finish and movement, and are pulled for privacy and as a shield against the sun.

Outside rooms confound the in-out distinction: a breezy outdoor pavilion connects to an interior breakfast room, with both areas running alongside the pool. The Morgans added a roof to this outside space, transforming an ordinary area into a sitting room off the boys' wing.

Above: The living area soars to twelve and a half feet. Ceilings in other rooms, including the foyer in back, are eight feet high.

Opposite: In the library, original dark paneling has been left to frame views and contrast with a new fireplace wall in travertine marble. Plush 1970s-vintage furniture surrounds a maple table in a classic amoeba shape. The rug is a mid-century favorite, a flokati—a soft, shaggy, handwoven woolen from Greece.

Ranch Style FURNITURE

Architect-designed furniture, such as the collection at left, was one of the glories of modernism. The chaise longue is an original made in 1928 of chromed tubular steel by Le Corbusier, Pierre Jeanneret, and Charlotte Perriand. Charles and Ray Eames designed the red Sofa Compact in 1954 with foam cushions and chrome-plated legs. The black vinyl chair, a 1950s Kroehler, was purchased at a garage sale, while the side and coffee tables are original Thonet, rescued when the local USO closed. On the table are Italian glasswork, an ebonized wood compote, and a Steuben Glass bowl. The shades are from a 1949 cantilevered Arteluce floor lamp by Gino Sarfatti. All the pieces are intended to be seen from 360 degrees.

Charles Eames, born in 1907 in St. Louis, is often considered the exemplar of twentieth-century American design. A standout trait of this architect was his great knowledge of production techniques and materials. "Technically brilliant, his work was characterized by pure colors, whimsical expression, lightness and mobility," note Kathryn B. Hiesinger and George H. Marcus in *Landmarks of Twentieth-Century Design*. While studying and teaching architecture at the prestigious Cranbrook Academy of Art in Bloomfield Hills, Michigan, he met two great future collaborators: Ray Kaiser (born in 1916), an artist whom he would marry; and fellow instructor Eero Saarinen.

With Saarinen, Charles worked on prototypes for molding plywood into complex curves for chairs, pursuing the plywood experiments during the war for the Navy. That work led to some of the Eameses' most important work, notably the Eames Chair, made of two pieces of molded plywood and joined with stainless steel tubing, and to their breakthrough in creating molded fiberglass chairs. Two of Charles Eames's greatest architectural achievements were for the Case Study program in California, which began in the mid-1940s, with Case Study #9 (1949, built with Eero Saarinen for the program's founder, John Entenza) and #8 (also 1949, built for himself and his wife, Ray).

With Sacramento-born Ray, an abstract artist who studied with Hans Hofmann, he influenced architecture, filmmaking, photography, communications, and the design of furniture, textiles, graphics, and toys. The California Office of Charles and Ray Eames aimed to mass-produce affordable, handsome designs that would enhance American lives. Highly creative, the pair was also extremely productive. They also created a seven-screen slide show for the 1959 Moscow World's Fair and, later, IBM's exhibition for the 1964–65 New York World's Fair. Their American Bicentennial exhibit traveled the world. Charles died on August 21, 1978; Ray died exactly ten years later.

Opposite: Inside, stretches of clear and bright light fill the house, while on the other side of the glass is the intensity of vibrating blues. Says Cindy Morgan, "It's very seductive." Below: Another play on space. A breakfast area feels as if it's both indoors and outdoors, literally framed by the outdoors and the ivy that surrounds the oversize full-height window. The Tulip table is by Eero Saarinen and the chairs by Harry Bertoia.

Above: The open room has a languorous feeling, with low-slung Afghani chairs and a daybed; the lamp is from India. The two spaces—one for napping, the other for sitting—give the room more options than simply being a poolside retreat.

Ranch Style CURVES

The victory in World War II took a strong nationalism to an even stronger new level, naturally spilling over into the home. As wartime technologies transferred to producing furniture in new ways (by machine, using molds) and in new forms of materials (fiberglass, plastics, molded plywood), the look of furniture changed, evincing bold, imaginative shapes. Curves, suggesting movement, were most influential: modeling science, curves showed up in amoeba and atomic shapes; space was reflected in parabolas and their derivative boomerang shapes, and in direct images of rockets and planes.

Above: Simplicity in all white, with living-room-worthy furniture (mahogany veneer table, art deco floor lamp), is for the Morgans' sophisticated teenage daughter. The flokati rug softens the concrete. Right: In the master bedroom, varied textures and finishes give neutrals star presence. The glamorous black steel 1930s bed was designed by Norman Bel Geddes. The 1950s bedside table and bookcases are lacquered wood. The mirror and Italian floor lamps together make a three-sided canopy. Concrete floors in the bedrooms add industrial contrast.

Ranch Style BEDROOMS

To make their daughter's room (above) seem taller, and to raise the stature of a basic bed, the Morgans tracked sets of simple white linen curtains on the ceiling all the way around the bed, pulling the back curtains closed to form a soft headboard. The bedspread is also linen. The same clean-lined drapery approach is applied at the glass doors and windows in all the bedrooms, including at these sliders that lead to the new palm court.

Left: From the living room, one step leads down to a classic conversation pit full of mid-century curves. A pair of 1950s apostrophe-shaped sofas are redressed from gold-and-green tweed to surprisingly glamorous white vinyl. A rounded chair is by Gilbert Rohde from the 1930s (Rohde was instrumental in bringing modern furniture to the American home, producing furniture for companies such as Herman Miller, Heywood-Wakefield, and Thonet). A warm slab of onyx lies over the top of the Eero Saarinen Tulip table, supporting Murano glass bottles. On the side table are a 1950s German clock and a white Alvar Aalto vase in one of Aalto's classic undulating shapes.

Below: A recently installed palm court brings new geography to the house. Through the arches in back is a step-down meditation courtyard with a raised koi pond.

early history lessons

1850s ROMANCE

Courtney Johnson Walker holds a sepia-toned photograph from the 1850s showing the three main buildings on a Texas ranch. The same three buildings are also right in front of her: a main house; a separate kitchen, which once isolated cooking heat as much as it did the realities of food preparation; and a smokehouse. In the center is a raised cistern.

The 150-year-old ranch was set up by a German immigrant family, following the path of similar settlers in the increasingly German-speaking Texas Hill Country. The parents, their nine children, and a set of grandparents ranched and

This photo, most likely taken in the late 1850s, displays (from the left) the main house, kitchen, and smokehouse. In the center is a limestone cistern for catching precious rain, often the sole water source for the entire needs of a family and their animals.

farmed the stubborn, stony earth. As it was a working ranch, there were other structures on the property, still standing: carriage house, large barn, stable, work sheds, and a series of corrals dotting hundreds of acres.

"Because timber was scarce," says Walker, "the buildings are all made of native fieldstone." And because summer heat could be punishing, ample central vents were installed to lure and snare great gulps of air. Roofs were pitched higher and steeper to circulate a breeze as long as possible. Eighteen-inch-thick walls insulated against scorching summer heat and surprisingly cold winters. The mortar for the stone walls was made in the local manner, of grass and native caliche, while the inside walls were plastered.

Walker's parents took over the ranch in 1950 from descendants of the settlers, and it became the Johnson family's weekend home. Walker, who has vivid girlhood memories of exploring every inch of the land and structures, now presides over it all, as well as over the Courtney &

Company design firm in San Antonio, of which she's president.

Walker connected the old smokehouse to adjoining sheds and workrooms, converting them all into her private home. She turned the other two main structures into their own fully functioning homes, opening them to her son and his wife and to her daughter's family. "Those two buildings were already linked by covered breezeways," Walker explains. "Now, all three houses are connected to one another, but we all have our own privacy." Visitors stay down the road a ways, in the carriage house, a space containing pool tables and full guest quarters.

"I feel very fortunate to have such a great sense of history here," says Walker. "Sometimes, when I'm in a room I particularly love, and I look through these old windows, I like to think about what they've seen and who's stood there over the years."

Previous page: One raised side of the pool serves as a wall for an outdoor dining room.

Ranch Style **TABLETOPS**

Cow vases, part of a collection of Staffordshire animals, are reminders of ranching and frame the dining area on the patio. "We often dine out here," says Walker. "I like the contrast of these fine items in a more primitive setting." The vintage white tablecloth adds old-time elegance. Atop old books is a collection of antique spice boxes that have exotic and artful graphics. The trophies, won by Walker's parents at horse shows, now make winning vases.

Right: Courtney Walker's residence, the old smokehouse, is at the far right. In back are some of the connecting passageways—many of them covered—linking the houses. The cistern has been converted into a swimming pool. "When you climb up the six steps to get in the pool—as opposed to stepping down, as you would in a traditional pool—you remember that this pool once served an important function," she points out. Below: Steeply pitched structures are found throughout ranches in the Hill Country. The stone houses were given new metal roofs and a sage green trim for unobtrusive contrast. A walled-off garden is exactly where it was in the late 1850s, and a welcoming front porch is formed by the classic long overhang.

Right: The entrance to Walker's residence is under a covered passageway. Original carved and etched-glass doors are found throughout the residences as exterior and interior doors. The rounded window was added during renovation.

Ranch Style BEDS

In a rare departure from antiques, the bamboo four-poster bed projects a relaxed, airy feeling. Bed linens accentuate the bamboo's natural tones and the emphasis on texture: the pillow fabric is Scalamandré silk and damask, some with a thick fringe trim; the duvet is intentionally simple, in soft white cotton; the delicate dust ruffle appears more substantive because it's two skirts, gauze over cotton. Straw hats, hanging from the posts, add another texture and soften the edges.

Below: "I love this fireplace so much that as soon as the season changes, I immediately get a fire going," says Walker. Her builder, James Seiter, formed it from stones found on the property. Hanging over it is a Mexican glass "pillow star" lamp, named for its soft, puffed quality.

Above: The soaring ceiling and nine-foot-tall doors add larger-than-life drama to the master bedroom. Arched window openings, original to the structure, were outfitted with casement windows for full-length breezes and vistas. Over the bed is a Robert Wade hand-painted photograph of Mexican rancheras in the 1930s. Ladylike, at the foot of the bed, is a scroll-back English hall chair.

Ranch Style FLOORS

Adding to the back-in-time feeling, the floors throughout the house are vintage, procured from the estate sale for the former Sullivan Carriage House in San Antonio. They are constructed with caliche bricks around a square wooden brick, forming an old-fashioned basket pattern. The unusual tones of the bricks are in part due to their previous life. "Creosote, a brownish oily liquid, was often poured on the brick floors of carriage houses to cut down on the horses' slipping," Walker explains. The color variations make the pattern subtler, and are reminders of the pavers' former workaday life.

Ranch Style ANTIQUES

In keeping with the owner's love of history, most of her furnishings were retrieved from the past. Filling the ledges are groupings of a Staffordshire donkey, Mexican pineapple ceramics, and vintage books, flanked by English horn lamps from the 1840s. The dignity in the comfortable space comes from rich, bold fabrics and the confident, squared lines of the furniture. The Empire sofa, re-covered in a dynamic, richly toned tapestry pattern, was Walker's mother's. Two high-backed armchairs were found at a garage sale and covered in vintage salmon-colored fabric. The side table between them is an old coal bin. The assortment of styles and periods holds together because of the furnishings' classic lines and because the collections have been kept controlled and clustered rather than scattered.

Below: Walker turned the central room of the old smokehouse into her living room. Behind the sofa are the original ledges used to hold meat that was being smoked and cured. The two small windows, fireplace, walls, and high-pitched roof are all original.

Above: In the kitchen, light pours in from an open set of glass French doors. Right: In the guestroom, a daybed is covered in black-and-white toile by Scalamandre, with checked pillows in Schumacher fabric. The American pastel artwork is early 1800s.

Ranch Style KITCHENS

A period look is achieved in the kitchen with a variety of vintage details. The old half-moon window and rescued marble (similar to the bathroom's) blend beautifully with cabinetry that was crafted from cast-off pine barn doors. The herringbone-pattern floor flows from adjoining rooms. Two iron doors, discovered in the barn, were incorporated into the French doors, functioning as beautiful screens.

Above: Sun-bleached animal horns hooked over a wood fence underscore the ranch setting. Below: The outdoor sitting room, with a roof consisting of cedar posts on a metal frame, anchors a corner of the patio. The owner's father designed the small coffee table: "The top comes off and inside is a copper box, so a fire can be built in it." Behind it all, pastures stretch to the horizon. Acknowledges Walker, "This is our favorite sitting spot."

SURF SHACK SHIMMY

"It's very Jetsons," fashion designer Cynthia Rowley remembers saying appreciatively to her husband, Bill Keenan, a sculptor and designer. "The overhang is very cool," he replied, upping the ante. This what-do-you-think transpired from the backseat of their broker's car, which was idling in front of the house as they peered intently out the window, smitten. No one in the car had a clue about the hidden value of what they were actually looking at.

All they saw, almost shimmering in the noontime light, was a house, purportedly built in 1946, with a very large, multipanel sliding glass door and a flat roof on a slight angle. It was supposedly one large room with a galley kitchen, but the interior was off-limits because it was rented. Rowley, nine months pregnant, gamely asked, "How bad could one room be?" Keenan reminded her that it was, after all, one block from the beach. Without getting out of the car, they said, "We'll take it."

And then it was theirs, all five hundred square feet, incognito in a surfing community on the South Fork of Long Island. They had wanted a shack by the beach to satisfy their surfing pursuits and to be the antithesis of their previous beach life—a million-dollar home on a white-glove street. They already had a Manhattan apartment, and they wanted this retreat to literally just need sweeping to be maintained. They ended up with something more.

Two years later, after renovations were complete, they learned that their little pad had been built by Donald Deskey, the designer of the interior of Radio City Music Hall in 1932. Deskey, in the fifties, designed the packaging for top-selling products such as Prell, Tide, and the Crest packaging still in use. Furthermore, the seemingly no-big-deal house had attended the 1939–1940 New York World's Fair, part of an industrial-design exhibit, billed as a prefabricated home. It had most likely been torn down after the fair and rebuilt at the beach.

Deskey had drawn the house to incorporate Weldtex, a new striated plywood that he designed specifically for this project, using the new material on the walls and ceilings. A fairground brochure predicted Rowley and Keenan's desire: "Easy to assemble: 'Sport Shack!' A new type of multipurpose house designed for modern living . . . for an all-year home, a hunting lodge . . . a beach house. . . ." Their surf shack was an architectural marvel.

Above: There was excitement about prefabricated construction when New York architect Donald Deskey made this 1940 design for weekend living called "Sport Shack." (Gouache, partially air brushed, stenciled, ink and graphite on illustration board; Cooper-Hewitt, National Design Museum, Smithsonian Institution/Art Resource, NY; Gift of Donald Deskey) Right: "This is a heavy-duty garage door," Keenan explains about the sliding multi-panel front door.

The magic of the Deskey house is that Rowley and Keenan responded to its architectural zing when it was more Cinderella than mid-century hallmark. Keenan, who always suspected that it was a prefabricated house, had also instinctively preserved and reused panels of the striated plywood during renovation. "They seemed advanced even for 1946," he remembers.

The optimism and vitality of the World's Fair is now built into their lives. Reclining on a rattan chair, toddler in her lap, Rowley says, "When we wake up and push aside the glass door, and our house opens completely to the outdoors, I feel like everything is fresh and possible. We get that feeling every single time."

Previous page: The view that Cynthia Rowley and Bill Keenan bought from inside a car. Coincidentally, a 1940s press clipping points out that the house could be had "at the price of a family car." The cost back then was $1,285 unassembled, though equipped and furnished.

Ranch Style WINDOWS

Picking up on the interior's nautical lighting theme, Keenan installed portholes on all the doors. For ease of installation, he used van windows from custom car shops, "which is why they're slightly tinted," he says.

By shifting the driveway to the opposite side of the house, the owners asserted the new studio status of the former garage—and inadvertently created a perfect view from the living room of Keenan's 1965 Galaxy convertible.

Ranch Style
WALLS AND CEILINGS

Weldtex was the name of the striated plywood invented by the United States Plywood Corporation for the Surfshack exhibit at the World's Fair. Resolutely strong, "it has a one-of-a-kind texture," Rowley notes. The intent was a rustic, sporty feeling. Deskey used Weldtex for the walls, prefabricated in four- by eight-foot sections, and the ceiling. Imaginatively, he also used it as a partition; punched with rows of circles, it allows air to move through the wall, cleverly redefining space and the views in and out of each hole. A pioneer designer, Deskey was also one of the first to use Bakelite, Formica, and brushed aluminum in his work.

Ranch Style
LIVING ROOMS

Inside is spontaneous fun: the striated-plywood ceiling and walls, painted creamy yellow, make a perfect container for a few lighthearted, easily movable furnishings. The sofa, a petite vintage Dux, was reupholstered in top-of-the-line tweedy green wool, and the rest of the room's décor came from garage sales, everything $3 or under. Behind the sofa, one of the interior porthole lights is visible. The yellow sculpture is by Keenan.

Ranch Style GUEST ROOMS

With the garage converted into Rowley's writing space (she is coauthor, with Ilene Rosenzweig, of *Swell Dressed Party,* on entertaining) and Keenan's studio, there remained the problem of a guest room. The solution: they pulled up a sleek 1969 Airstream and parked it in back of the house. The trailer is referred to by aficionados as a land yacht: crafted from aircraft-grade Alclad aluminum, these complete homes-on-wheels were made for happily rolling down the new highway system of the 1950s and 1960s. "It's perfectly self-contained, like the house," says Rowley. "Guests are thrilled when we tell them it's all theirs."

Right: The bedroom is pared down to basics: a bed and a small table. The soothing, retro design of the bedcover and of the house in general were the inspiration for owner Cynthia Rowley's bed-linen designs. Below: A unique guest house. Today Airstreams are coveted examples of modernist industrial design—just like the house. The feeling of a compound is achieved with a stone path that leads to the garage and curves around to the Airstream trailer.

Low-slung rattan chairs and lounge-able pillows are the only porch furnishings. Similarly, interior accessories are few but key.

Ranch Style ARCHITECTURE

"I don't know if it's the ultimate ranch house, but it's the smallest," muses owner Rowley. The house's architect, Minnesota-born Donald Deskey, studied in Paris and then was based in New York. But the influence of California modernists is apparent in everything from the flat roof to the big overhang. Under "Assembly Instructions," the brochure for the house boasts that once the slab was poured, the house "[could] be erected in three to five days!" The couple planted yucca to play up the West Coast flair.

Opposite: Because space is tight, "we had to keep furnishings to a bare minimum," says Rowley. Right: By day, this space is a study. At night, a foldable bed turns it into a bedroom for the owners' daughter. The size of the holes in the original 1939 partition closely matches the size of the porthole lights, maintaining a simple and strong theme. Below: At dusk, the interior and exterior porthole lights come on, combining the two spaces even with the door closed. The yellow paint in the main room turns gold, and the inner sliding door takes on a watery glisten. "We're totally relaxed when we're here," says Rowley.

A NEW RIFF ON CLIFF MAY

"The sound of rain on this roof will mesmerize you," says Dianne Parker, an abstract painter. "One of the layers of roof materials is ground porcelain, and when rain hits it, it's an incredible sound, like feet crunching on the beach. It feels unique to this house."

Even with a modest budget, she and her husband, Scott, an architect, had dreamed of living in a home by acclaimed modernist Richard Neutra, Rudolph Michael Schindler, or Craig Ellwood. Instead, they found themselves traipsing through bland houses until providence winked when they came across this Cliff

May house outside Long Beach, California. Often called the father of ranch-style living, May is noted for combining the western ranch house and Hispanic hacienda styles with elements of modernism. Later, May began designing homes that were pure modernism. Both styles of his work helped set off the wave of California ranches that Americans fell in love with.

The classic L-shaped 1954 structure that the Parkers bought was in a tract of a hundred Cliff May houses, and it was a modern style, satisfying Scott's preference. Surprisingly, it had an affordable price tag because it was badly run-down and had been empty for a year. It was also only thirteen hundred square feet. But Dianne loved the generous light, and Scott saw the chance to own a part of architectural history.

Previous page: The sage green exterior with white trim casually dignifies the pedigree. The three-bedroom, two-bath redwood house is set to the very back of its lot in order to leave a large yard, a placement seen in many of Frank Lloyd Wright's Usonian homes. The owners used square two-foot pavers, filled in with ⅜-inch pea gravel, to create a geometric grid.

They removed the seventies-era kitchen and a tiny fourth bedroom, and had the house ripped down to its studs, revealing a wood-frame system that was doweled together with pegs. "I love the structural logic of the house," explains Scott, a partner at Johnstone Parker Architects in Gardena, California. "There is five and a half feet from the center of one post to the center of the next, all the way around the house," he says, "making a modular frame."

The Parkers tried to restore the house as close to its original condition as possible. On a limited budget, the couple did a lot of the renovation themselves, over a period of two and a half years.

"That first night in bed, I looked up, through the clerestory window, which I had never thought much about, and moonlight came into the bedroom," Scott remembers. "I was seeing it in a new way, which was May's intent, and it was a transformative experience. I looked over at Dianne, who was asleep, and some of the moonlight was touching her, and I thought, '*This* is how you're supposed to live.'"

"With California ranch houses, Cliff May and others just had to add water and stir—it was like California in a container," observes Daniel Gregory, Ph.D., an architectural historian and a home editor at *Sunset* magazine in Menlo Park, California, referring primarily to California's offerings of a temperate climate, indoor-outdoor living, and a lifestyle that embraced informality. When *Sunset* discovered May in 1933, he was developing his adaptation of 1830s and 1840s haciendas "and adding modern elements such as having the house and patio on one level, without steps between," says Gregory of a style that the California elite and middle class commissioned from May.

By the late 1940s and 1950s, May was designing an additional style of ranch house. "Any modernist influence would have to come to him indirectly by way of the young graduates of the University of Southern California School of Architecture he brought into his office—Chris Chaote, William F. Cody, and Jack Lester," comments David Bricker in *Toward a Simpler Way of Life*. Those modernist influences came especially into play "when May got into the development business," says Gregory from the Cliff May–designed *Sunset* offices. While May personally designed more than 1,000 commissions, "his designs for low-cost ranch homes were used in the construction of at least 18,000 houses built by licensed contractors after the end of World War II," writes Marlene L. Laskey in "The California Ranch House" for the Oral History Program at University of California in Los Angeles.

Opposite: A modern Cliff May home from the fifties. (From *Western Ranches* by Cliff May, courtesy Hennessey & Ingalls) Below: Raised ceilings are key to most of May's work, whether a modern home such as this one or a rancho style.

Above: Fifties birch chairs were re-covered in a tight sage-and-beige swirl. A reproduction 1946 George Nelson slatted platform bench, for Herman Miller, refines the look. Left: The casual entry has a simple concrete threshold. Opposite: An homage to the wall-mounted cabinets designed by architects such as Marcel Breuer, Scott conceived this one in maple plywood to house stereo equipment. Above is one of Dianne's artworks.

Ranch Style FIREPLACES

The fireplace wall had been a hodgepodge of brick and drywall. To add drama and to simplify the materials, the owners added a broad plaster wall that reaches almost but not quite to the ceiling. In the top, they concealed indirect fluorescent lights to project a soft, diffused glow. The hearth's brick was covered in black slate to ground the space. The hand-troweled, unadorned green wall lends texture and solidity to the airiness of the room.

Ranch Style **KITCHENS**

The focus of the open kitchen is the suspended custom hood, designed by Scott to be as open as possible and to echo the living room's floating cabinet. The hood, counters, and cabinets are made of maple plywood, less expensive than solid wood. In another cost-saving move, some storage is open, with glass shelves.

Because the key to successful mid-century style is a consistent, flowing approach, particular attention is paid to carry that message through the kitchen's workstation. The owners were faithful to materials (maple plywood) and to colors (black, white, and metal tones). Maple-plywood cabinetry from the living room continues into the kitchen (maple is even used for the backsplash), linking the spaces and giving the kitchen a furnished feeling.

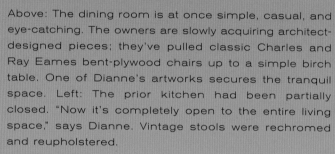

Above: The dining room is at once simple, casual, and eye-catching. The owners are slowly acquiring architect-designed pieces; they've pulled classic Charles and Ray Eames bent-plywood chairs up to a simple birch table. One of Dianne's artworks secures the tranquil space. Left: The prior kitchen had been partially closed. "Now it's completely open to the entire living space," says Dianne. Vintage stools were rechromed and reupholstered.

Ranch Style **OPEN PLANS**

Instead of a traditional foyer, the entrance is through the French doors (next to the fireplace) and immediately into the radical open-plan great room. The pitched ceilings make each room feel airier, rising nine and a half feet and covered with original square insulation panels. "We left the panels because they give a nicer rhythm to the room than a solid expanse would," Scott Parker explains. The exposed beams are seen in many of May's houses, adding to the frankness of construction.

Right: A glass corner creates a space that has an atrium effect. The Eames lounge chair and ottoman are in tune with the natural palette of the house.

Below: "I love the French doors off our bedroom," says Dianne. "In the summer, cross-ventilation brings in fragrances from the courtyard plantings. It's a breath of heaven."

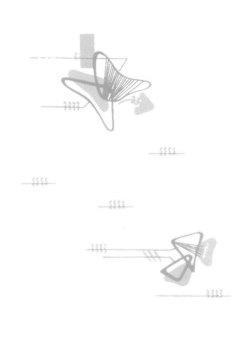
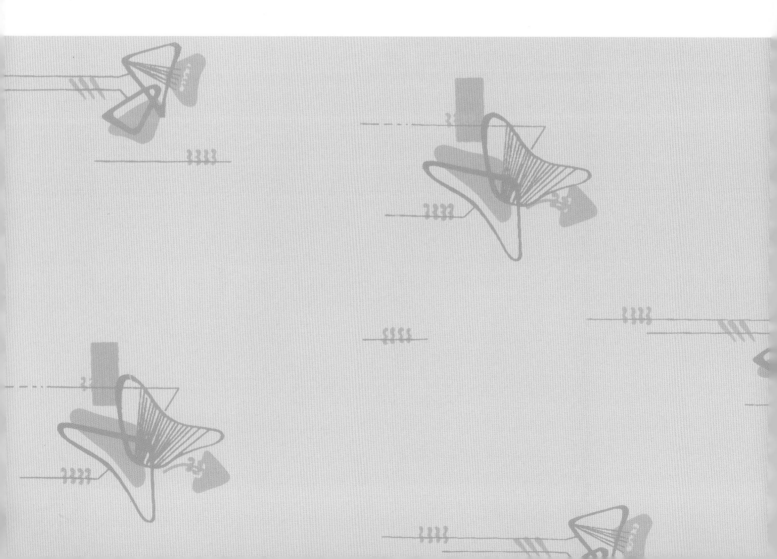

style changes

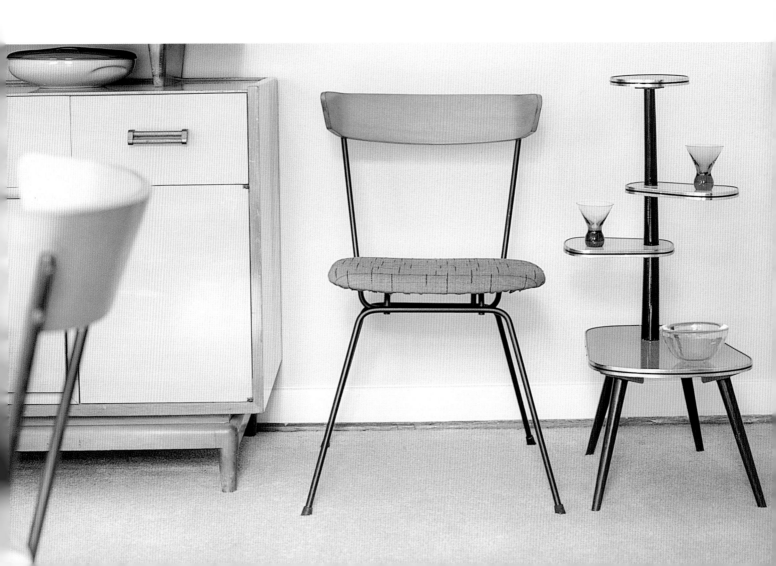

GROOVY THING GOING ON

Rick Marin and Ilene Rosenzweig remember the stunned look on Hamptons real estate agents' faces when they'd cheerfully announce, "We'd like to look at ranches." They didn't have to suffer those expressions for long. The couple, style writers and editors at *The New York Times*, fell for the very first ranch they saw.

The 1954 house, in New Haven, New York, possessed everything they were looking for in a country-house escape from Manhattan. It had a traditional Hamptons shingled exterior and plenty of space in a classic three-bedroom, two-bath arrangement. At fifteen hundred square feet, the house's intimate scale was a warm fit. It appealed to Rick's sixties sensibility, and it felt right to Ilene, who had grown up in a ranch.

Their first date two years earlier had been at a party held at the Sunset Beach Hotel on nearby Shelter Island. So when their real estate agent turned slowly onto Sunset Road, they couldn't help but lock eyes and think, Where's the contract?

The last owner had already made important renovations, cleaning up the line of the interior and building a deck in back. Without blueprints, it's unclear whether the lifted roofline is original, though it was most likely made by a subsequent resident. This clever, simple detail raised the ceiling above the kitchen, adding height and light from an eye-catching strip of windows. Equally important, this angled tier, still in keeping with the mood of the house, adds complexity and curb appeal.

With the bones of the house already in order, Ilene and Rick put their energy into pop sixties and seventies styling. "We wanted to keep the cool aspects of the house and make it feel fresh rather than old and musty," says Ilene. Adds Rick, "There's a fine line between staying true to a period and living in the past, and we want the inspiration but not necessarily the exact look."

Together they furnished the house with pieces from mid-century stores in downtown Manhattan, business trips to Chicago and Los Angeles, and weekend road trips to New Jersey. Their theme for the house, unspoken at first, was inevitable: plenty of lighthearted fun in the . . . sun.

A single piece of furniture and a few large artworks make a clean and dramatic first impression. The upholstered steel-frame chair is Harry Bertoia's influential bent-wire 1952 Diamond lounge chair. The mounted black-and-white picador poster came from a sidewalk vendor.

Ranch Style BERTOIA CHAIRS

Because of the ranch's built-ins and the mind-set of paring down, rooms had less furniture and the chair became a star. One of the most influential designers was Harry Bertoia, an American sculptor and designer originally from Italy. During his career, Bertoia collaborated with Charles Eames and worked at a defense plant where Eames was a research director; he also helped develop Charles and Ray Eames's plywood techniques. After the war, Bertoia moved to Pennsylvania and teamed with Florence and Hans Knoll, developing the classic Diamond lounge chair in 1951 and 1952, made out of a steel grid that is bent, welded with steel rods, and then attached to a metal stand. The chair came in polished chrome or nylon coating.

Previous page: The streamlined 1972 Cutlass convertible is right at home, as is the sleek, upward-looking roofline that adds pep to an otherwise classic L shape. Also simple, just a pair of beautiful, oversize boxwoods, original to the house, makes for a modern look.

Right: Turn on the hi-fi: "STEREO. A Two-Channel recording . . . " Below: Outdoor themes fill the house, here in a vintage Italian vase ringed with flower-power colors. The sweetly perched glass bird statue, in a favorite sixties pair-up of gold with plastic, reminded Rick Marin of Woodstock and his childhood *Peanuts* obsession.

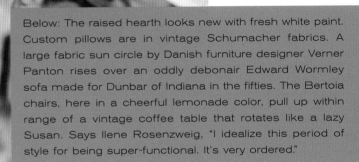

Below: The raised hearth looks new with fresh white paint. Custom pillows are in vintage Schumacher fabrics. A large fabric sun circle by Danish furniture designer Verner Panton rises over an oddly debonair Edward Wormley sofa made for Dunbar of Indiana in the fifties. The Bertoia chairs, here in a cheerful lemonade color, pull up within range of a vintage coffee table that rotates like a lazy Susan. Says Ilene Rosenzweig, "I idealize this period of style for being super-functional. It's very ordered."

Above: A brazen molten saturation of red: the Finnish glass vase is Riihimaen Lasi Oy. Below: Ready for spontaneous conversation: 1969 Plia chairs by Giancaria Piretti in steel and polypropylene. Vintage stereo cabinet is now a full-service cocktail counter.

Above: Pillow talk is conducted on a plastic and laminate bed set. Red rules in Spanish artist Sonia Soms's silk screens, the window-pane sheeting, and inflatable pillows. The lamp came from a former Playboy Club. Opposite: Photos of family and friends—plus one of Regis Philbin—are autographed with tongue-in-cheek tributes to their hosts. The wall was inspired by celebrity headshots in New York restaurants. Below : A thirteen-and-a-half-foot ceiling and a Plexiglass chandelier brighten the kitchen.

ZEN AND THE ART OF HAMPTONS LIVING

"It starts the moment I make the turn off Main Street, especially in the summer when it's packed here. It's all about decompression. I make that turn, and the atmosphere already becomes freer and less crazy, as if you can feel the air start to come out of your tires," says Cee Scott Brown. "When I reach my street, there's a definite sense of fulfillment about coming home. This house is a retreat, very Zen-like and quiet."

One of the Hamptons' top-tier real estate agents, Brown has structured his Sag Harbor, New York, home in a form of "less is more" that mirrors a piece of art he hung opposite his bed: By Jenny Holzer, the plaque reads, "Protect me from what I want."

Brown was one of the few people who responded to the house. Built in the late thirties, it had most recently been home to a pair of artists who had lived there for fifty years, neglecting the house and amassing piles of art and paraphernalia that filled floor and air space. "People were put off by its condition, and they wanted amenities for an asking price that they thought was too high," he remembers. "I loved the openness, the high ceilings and the funky porch, and the water views. And I loved that it had a history. Elia Kazan rented it in the fifties. John Steinbeck lived next door—Elaine, his wife, still does."

The house was small—eleven hundred square feet—but the living room's eighteen-foot peak and the eight-and-a-half-foot-tall ceilings in the other rooms could lead toward something wonderful. Brown named his new environment after one of Steinbeck's books and Kazan's movies, *East of Eden*.

Brown's completed vision is full of surprises, from the unexpected Asian overtones to unforeseen landscaping jewels. Despite its previous state, the house was left intact—cleaning up was a matter of paint, giving the inside a whitewash and the outside a dark neutral to cover pinkish beige. The already closed-in porch received three changes: mismatched jalousie windows were replaced with multipaned sliders to take full advantage of breezes; windows were installed near the door; and cedar planks were added to match the interior walls.

Landscaping received the rest of the attention. Brown even installed a tall privet hedge that completely obscures the house from the street, a strategy that could be questioned: In this status-conscious scene, why be tucked away, why hide that you are on the water? "I like surprises." He shrugs. "I like to be in an unassuming position."

Previous page: To someone motoring in by boat, the ranch-house form, edged with tiers of beach grass, is clear. This is the front of the house: "I loved the view from the water," remembers Cee Scott Brown of his first visit, "how the house nestled into the landscape."

The path leads to a corner of the lawn, where a well-placed invitation to relax is slung between two trees. The walkway is packed stone dust to give the quiet, padded feeling of a beaten path.

Ranch Style LANDSCAPING

The grounds are a large part of the house's new appeal—as can often be the case with ranches, with their emphasis on indoor-outdoor flow and harmony between architecture and land. Owner Brown, along with landscape designers Joseph Cornetta in Water Mills, New York, and Douglas Reed in Watertown, Massachusetts, formed three bands of plantings. The first is the wetland plantings, running along the waterfront, and includes bayberry, dune grasses, fragrant sumac, rugosa roses, and *Phragmites australis*. Across the back of the house is the second band—an overflowing bed of perennials. Near the hammock, and leading to the water, are the woodland plantings such as autumn olives, viburnums, and hydrangeas. Color consultant Donald Kaufman recommended the darker paint to help blend the house into its surroundings.

Ranch Style **DECKS**

"When you see the water for the first time, you're ready to receive that image of the Buddha," explains Brown of the Balinese icon that reflects his extensive travels to Indonesia and Japan. Adding to the peacefulness, the deck is meant to appear as a raft floating on the water, with exposed, curved supports that impart a sense of lightness. Instead of traditional steps, large stones add naturalness. "The wonderful thing about living on the water is that the view changes every hour of every day. And since the house is the frame for that view, I prefer a simple, functionary frame that makes for a peaceful home. I don't like huge statements."

In back of the house, entirely shielded from the street by a tall privet hedge, the entrance to the yard allows this view. The cottage-style perennial bed aims for an overgrown look, with plantings in bloom year-round.

The living room has soaring dimensions, a feeling sustained by the sofa's white canvas, with the other furniture in dark finishes. The pair of artist studio tables were found at a yard sale. Textured lamps, from Nantucket, have twine-over-parchment shades and a rope pole. The chandelier was found at a tag sale. French club chairs are from the early 1900s.

Opposite: Brown utilizes the porch as a dining room. "You can tell that the room was outside at one time, then enclosed. There's something nice about that," he says. A mix of styles and periods helps create the serene, worldly atmosphere in every room. Semigloss white paint was used throughout the house on walls and ceilings. Wood floors here and in the living room were painted with black-green deck stain. Above: Reinforcing the natural tones, the grooved plates are contemporary Japanese ceramics, the runner is an Indonesian woven floor mat, and the elephant vase is from Thailand. The tall blue-and-green vase is by artist Joan Bankemper.

Ranch Style PERIOD PIECES

A few well-chosen, iconoclastic pieces lend a period mood. The freestanding lamp is Akari, by Isamu Noguchi, based on traditional Japanese folding lanterns, in mulberry-bark paper, bamboo, and wire. The 1950s wishbone chairs, made of wood and twine, and dining table, in steel and wood, show the Asian influences on Danish designer Hans J. Wegner. The antique hanging Japanese lantern, in black, centers the space.

Rather than replace the kitchen, Brown left it intact, from the window trim to the off-white Formica counters. Originally he scrubbed the counters with steel wool, inadvertently taking off the finish and ending up with a matte patina that he likes and maintains.

Off the living space is a comfortable outdoor room shielded on three sides by greenery. The owner mixes wooden and metal chairs in a reprise of the interior's material. The large outdoor coffee table is Balinese teak on top of a rice table.

Ranch Style COLOR

To give the kitchen a calm, clean presence, the owner chose a monochromatic look. He used white paint in a high-gloss finish for ease of cleanup and its sheen, making the room appear larger. He painted the entire kitchen, including the inside of drawers and cabinets as well as the hinges and handles, to reduce visual clutter.

Ranch Style LINOLEUM

The floor in the bathrooms, kitchen, and bedrooms is standard linoleum squares. "I like the democratic nature of it; it's not elitist," says the owner. He chose it for its resemblance to stone—a putty brown color with streaks of black, salmon, and white. What gives it additional character is how it is arranged: tiles are laid so that the grains flow in one direction instead of being in a checkerboard effect. "I could achieve a more vintage look by having the floor appear to be a sheet of material rather than individual tiles."

Ranch Style BEDROOMS

Original casement windows and screens are found in the master bedroom, wide open in the morning. "I like the feeling of air circulating through the house—it's freeing," Brown explains. A simple shade is pulled at night. The bureaus are 1940s metal office cabinets, painted in tones of putty to mimic wood, with original mirrors. The hat-shaped lamps, also from the 1940s, were found individually, one in silver tones, one in brass. "I love that they're similar but not the same," he says. A simple white waffle-weave spread drapes the metal-frame bed; to avoid corrosion from salt air, the bed was nickel-plated.

Neutral hues and unusual materials give the bathroom singularity: a vintage medical cabinet creates highly useful storage, a white casement window opens up the room, and the light is a boating fixture.

The bedroom walls and ceiling have their original planking.

FIFTIES COOL

A highly regarded art restorer in the West had already looked at ten houses during her lunch-hour hunts. The best she had seen in her range were cramped, faux bungalow styles. She wanted a structure with integrity, not pretense. And as a single mother of two young children, she needed a house they'd be comfortable in.

When she and her broker pulled up in front of this classic three-bedroom, two-bath, 1956 ranch, she was not impressed. "I saw a standard, run-of-the-mill fifties house in a ranch-house community, and it was not my taste," she remembers. But since they were there, it wouldn't hurt to look, to gauge the market.

They entered through the kitchen, and the first thing they saw were large round cabinet knobs. "The broker said, 'You can change those, of course.' But I started to laugh just looking at them and said, 'No! They're amazing!' I couldn't believe anything could be so bold. I was getting intrigued." One spin and she was sold.

"The most beautiful part is the flow. It's so easy for raising children because there are large public spaces and a private wing of bedrooms. Now, with the children ready for college, the house works beautifully. Even though we're not in the same conversation, we can be with one another in the same general space."

Multiple entries to main rooms—a way of eliminating hallways and helping create flow—strikes her in another fashion: "It also means vistas that carry you from one room to the next."

Her sensitivity to the house was apparent from the beginning. "I restore modern art, so I suppose it's also my inclination where my home is concerned. I felt that the house was very proud. And so much of it was intact that I wanted to respect as much about it as I could, so that I could give it back what it had before. I never made a change just for the sake of it, and in fact I made very few changes. I tried to listen to the house. For instance, the windows are very low, and that sets up certain proportions in the rooms—with low sills, low furniture works best. The top of the chairs looks beautiful in this setting."

The house is so retro-stylish that there's the mark of a very restrained, very hip interior designer, which causes the owner to smile: "It's almost all flea-market purchases or hand-me-downs, chosen from the start because they're durable and spill-proof.

"These houses were about family living, and that's entirely the story here. If you walked in here in 1956, the house would look very much the same, and the mood would be similar, because it's young-hearted. That can be one of the wonderful parts of living in a fifties ranch."

Previous page: "The house comes alive at night," says the owner. Down-lights under the eaves make the brick glow and add sophisticated shadowing. To the right, a richly painted interior takes on assertive glamour.

The owner chose teal and dark green to showcase a mid-century love of geometrics in the raised trim and as rich complements to the brick. She continued the color to the porch ceiling to create the feeling of a room. In the modern 1950s, positioning a knob in the center of the door connoted new, "glam," and exciting. The knob is in the star shape that reflects the era's fondness for space and infinity.

Ranch Style LIGHTING

All of the lighting connotes mid-century icons. Behind the sofa, the French "marshmallow" standing floor lamp—found at a secondhand store—brings to mind not only the ubiquitous lamp shades (in parchment, leather, or plastic, almost always hem-stitched in leather, cord, or twine) but also George Nelson's playful 1956 Marshmallow sofa. On the far wall are two table lamps—on the left in hemp and straw, on the right in metal—both using fashionable reflective light and both very flying-saucer in the way of popular fixtures by George Nelson and A. W. & Marion Geller. Similar fixtures were the rage in France at the time. With the combination of diffused lighting, says the owner, "I love it at night."

Ranch Style FURNITURE

The languid, stretching curve of the boomerang-shaped sofa is a direct invitation to linger. Even so, "there is nothing pretentious in this room," notes the owner. She recovered the long sofa in aqua vinyl with black piping to show off its lines and to give it the feeling of a smart 1950s suit. "My son and daughter can sit eight on it," she says, "drinking soda and eating pizza." Short metal-tipped legs are typical of the 1950s and 1960s. Keeping the low profile are the sleek easygoing chrome and green-vinyl chairs—looking much like automobile seats—which came from an Ann Arbor, Michigan, dentist's office. The new amoeba-shaped coffee table, by artist William Steen, supports a Red Wing vase.

The living room conveys a calm, comfortable mood, assisted by a large floor-to-ceiling picture window that pours in soft light and vistas. On the back wall, works by three artists punctuate the space: from the left, German architect Werner Ruhnau, Californian Jay De Feo, and Fernand Léger. The box is by artist James Reaben.

Ranch Style COLOR

Rich color gives the living room vitality and forms a bolder backdrop for the furniture to play against. "Reddish terracotta and the ocher give the walls differing dimensions," says the owner. The fireplace is painted white to set up

three distinct areas on one wall for art. Adding background softness is the flat-weave gray wall-to-wall carpet.

Opposite: Gray and honey colors are an important part of the soothing, weightless feeling of the dining room, with walls in a light gray paint custom-mixed with extra yellow for warmth. The blond-wood Danish table was made in the 1960s and opens to seat twelve. Overhead, the ceiling fixture provides gravitational pull. In back, the small, curvy 1950s wood table is faced with black and gray Formica and accessorized with a chrome art-deco shaker, crumb tray, and brush. The art is by William Steen.

Above: The Swedish wood bureau becomes a vehicle for art: on the surface, a piece by James Reaben; above, by William Steen. The brushed-aluminum lamp is by Leviton. A 1930s candelabra adds drama.

Ranch Style PERIOD PIECES

The 1950s dining chairs are by furniture designer Paul McCobb, known for clean-lined pieces. McCobb's line brought affordable, well-designed furniture to the public through department stores, and his work was shown in the Museum of Modern Art's "Good Design" exhibitions, winning numerous times in the fifties. He is also known for his Planner Group, a low-priced line started in 1950 featuring birch and maple furnishings in simple shapes.

Above: The kitchen receives natural light most of the day from glass bricks located at a corner under the cabinets and from a large set of casement windows. Opposite: Wood paneling, in superb condition, adds a warm coziness. The 1950s American furniture is by Heywood-Wakefield, a company that counted Russel Wright and Gilbert Rohde among its designers. The table is set with highlights of collections that the owner uses every day.

Typical of well-built 1950s homes, a bathroom meant to be shared would be spacious. The combination of turquoise and pink tiles is original to the house. The simple turquoise sconce is reflected in the practical and indulgent four-sided mirror, even providing an overhead view. The vintage jewelry is by Matisse, Renoir of California; the petal bowl is by Catalina.

Ranch Style KITCHENS

The impossibly proud knobs, which measure a surprising five inches across, are an eye-catching period detail. Against original white tile, the maple-plywood cabinetry combines for a fresh look. "I kept the room spare to celebrate the extraordinary cabinetry," says the owner. "I love all the built-ins and pullouts—fifties cabinetry feels very custom."

The open feeling, minus even a small work island, is purposeful. "Everyone gathers here, and we like to sit on the counters with our legs dangling." Adding to the open feeling is the floor that she laid herself, replacing a busy and dark original; white linoleum squares are interspersed with a few in turquoise, ocher, and gray.

Ranch Style COLLECTIONS

From the classic sun clock by Howard Miller to the intergalactic toothpick holder, happiness in design is uninhibited. Collections of spirited vintage pieces can create or complete atmosphere, particularly in the kitchen, preferably in use. Here, a cookie-jar collection begins with a bear holding court at the table, by McCoy, 1953. On the counter, the bear is a rare turnabout—the other side of its face is a pout—by Ludowici Celadon. The pig cookie jars and salt and pepper shakers are by Shawnee, USA. The square dishes are from Franciscan; ribbed platters and bowls, by Bauer; gravy boat, by Fiesta.

FRENCH COTTAGE

They're living in a dream world, friends privately thought when the homeowners proclaimed that they were turning their drab ranch into a French cottage. They had been enticed by the half-acre-plus of land, angled on a hill for privacy.

The modest 1,750-square-foot house, built in 1954, also had practical components such as a bona fide foyer, eat-in kitchen, pantry, and mudroom. "The house was as plain as it could get," says the wife, "more like a shell, so it was ready for personality to be added." They hit upon the idea of French-country toile, combined with Indonesian accents to give it global sophistication.

Since a low budget was the reality, there would be no structural changes. Exterior and landscaping adjustments would have to adhere to the theme.

Inside, lighting was the first order of business, replacing dim relics with high-wattage fixtures in modern styling to make the country theme feel vibrant. Then the couple maximized the decorative potential of the walls with wallpaper, chair rails, and paint. Outside, the house underwent a facelift when cream-colored paint covered the charcoal blue shingles and red-orange brick. White trim provided clean lines that added to the effect. Narrow porch steps were extended, and a front patio was installed.

For landscaping, the owners sought professional advice, completely redoing the grounds. Joseph Cornetta of Water Mill, New York, and Charles Marder, of Bridgehampton, New York, extended the house's theme with orchards, installing a tall, graceful espaliered apple tree on one side and designating three pear trees for the other.

The entire effect is subtle and unexpected, slowly building to a French-cottage theme. Stepping through the new entry, the husband says, "Even I can't believe we did it."

Above: Setting up an orchard theme is a ten-foot-tall apple tree. The creamy exterior with white trim has a tranquil flow and creates a fresh and clean look.

The stucco garage wall is turned into something special, a perfect backdrop for espallered pear trees.

Ranch Style **LANDSCAPING**

Charles Marder, president of Marders, centered a stately, espaliered apple tree in a new bed (opposite, top). Developed centuries ago in France, an espalier—a plant pruned and trained to a flat pattern—is ideal for adding architectural interest, especially to narrow spaces. With it, left to right, are greenthread false cypress, rose of Sharon, burning bush, cherry laurel, hydrangeas, holly, dwarf lilac, dwarf asters, and Hinoki cypress. Above, landscape designer Joseph Cornetta used the garage wall as a canvas for three, rather than one, espaliers. "There is strength in repetition," he says. These pear trees are palmette verrier, a classic candelabra design named after nineteenth-century French agriculturalist Louis Verrier. Nepeta and 'Hidcote' lavender round out the theme.

Taking advantage of the shape of the private setback, the patio feels like a sheltered room. The owners put in simple raised beds and installed trellises for climbing roses; here, 'High Hopes' roses make a showing, inter-mingling with pink 'New Dawn' and 'White Dawn'. Pink begonias flop over the beds for more soft pink color.

In the rambling yard that is classic ranch house, a gar-den continues the new cottage mood: orange lilies, blue and purple delphiniums, blue and white veronica, and pink scabiosa. Delicate stalks of delphinium are showpieces in cottage gardens.

Ranch Style PATIOS

Overgrown bushes reaching to the tops of the windows were pulled out; a slate patio was installed and rimmed with river rocks. Large walking stones were spaced farther apart and interstices filled with the same river rocks for continuity. The front porch repeats the off-white and stone palette. Originally the first two steps had been only two feet wide. The owners had them stretched to the width of the slate porch, imparting much-needed dignity and increased access. River rocks were attached (using masonry glue) to mask the concrete risers and to provide unusual interest. Simple planters in concrete (rather than contrasting terra-cotta) continue the off-white theme and are filled with classic boxwoods.

The planting at the far end of the walk is given special consideration for impact, to stop the view and usher the eye toward the house.

A new gentility about the porch is due in part to the creamy paint. Instead of the traditional custom of painting all the house trim white, here only the windows, shutters, and a few pieces of trim are white. The rest of the house is cream—including the porch ceiling —making the walls appear taller and the porch bigger.

Ranch Style FOYERS

Foyers not only make the first impression, they define the house's style, acting as a decorating statement in miniature. Originally the room was a plain, Sheetrocked box. First, for an architectural element, a simple chair rail was installed, and a warm beige was painted underneath to brighten the space. Establishing the French theme, sage-and-ecru toile de Jouy wallpaper was applied above the rail; like all the wall details, it moves across the closet door for an unbroken pattern and to make the room feel larger. The wallpaper was then given ribbon molding (applied with clear caulk). A small polyurethane dome was installed to add a quirky grand note and to distinguish the intimate room. The mini-chandelier was chosen for its scale.

Opposite: In the foyer, the theme of off-whites and greens is gracefully carried inside. Right: Toile de Jouy, in warm green and raspberry tones, brings fresh interest to a small square room.

Ranch Style TOILE DE JOUY

In 1770, in a French village called Jouy-en-Josas, near Versailles, a German industrialist named Christophe-Philippe Oberkampf had one of the most successful factories for producing colorfast engravings on silk, cotton, and linen, satisfying the French desire for printed cottons that was stirred by fabrics brought over from India. Achieved with the use of copper plates, the intricate engravings often showed classical, floral, and pastoral scenes, the most renowned of which were in a single color on a light background. The prints his factory turned out were of such high caliber that "toile de Jouy" (*toile* meaning "fabric" or "cloth," and "Jouy" for the village's abbreviation) continues to be associated with fine textiles in that style.

Ranch Style DOORS

When the foyer was complete, the former, simple door could not hold its own. The owners looked for over a year, finding a possibility halfway across the country during a business trip to Texas. The door, with a leaded-glass panel depicting the torch of knowledge, had in 1890 belonged to the chancellor at the University of Texas. A local lumber company, through their custom department, sent someone to evaluate the door; the company could enlarge or diminish it to fit, as well as repair, pack, and ship it. "In general, we've found that there's greatest success if we make the door oversized for the existing frame," advises Greg L. Scott, of Stripling Blake Lumber Company in Austin, "so that the installer has room to maneuver." At the bottom of the door is a curved piece called a drip ledge that the owners had made; typical in Provence, the drip ledge keeps rain from gathering under the door. Here, it's added to the inside for effect.

Small tin lanterns ring the sitting room, adding dimension and atmosphere. At night, the pendant lamp is dimmed and the lanterns create a tentlike effect.

Ranch Style KITCHENS

The kitchen was left intact—the owners added just a fresh eye and a few cosmetic changes. The original curvy panel above the sink announces the 1950s and adds endearing softness. Red cross-hatch Formica counters from 1953 were kept for their cheer. The upper cabinets are adaptations of the originals: first, the doors were removed; plybead and a horizontal support were added between the shelves; and standard outer-corner trim was added to the front edge of each shelf and to the inside edge of the cabinet box. Consequently, the room automatically feels larger without cabinet doors. The lower cabinets were painted, and the handles were replaced with glinting new stainless steel. A few changes were made for practicality: a more convenient gooseneck faucet was added; the pot rack over the stove solves storage problems and adds coziness. For unexpected elegance, toile de Jouy makes a subtle appearance as a simple kitchen shade, and gold ballroom chairs impart a casual formality (albeit purchased inexpensively from a banquet company). Pulling in an Indonesian mood is the rugged mountain-grass rug.

The 1950's kitchen underwent a simple transformation into a warm room in the cottage style. This cabinet took only half a day to restructure. Its openness puts mugs and glasses in easy reach, while baskets hold odds and ends.

Ranch Style **TABLETOPS**

The table reflects the house's themes and unusual, spare sophistication. Instead of a tablecloth, a white sheet is casually knotted at each end, with a beach mat smoothed across the top. Circular straw mats support triangles of antique napkins. Interpreting the front landscaping, miniature iron topiaries brought back from the Palais Royal park in Paris stand alongside Waterford goblets. Calla lilies in a simple glass vase complete the effect.

Now a spacious dining room, the former living-room area is used frequently. Walls are sage green to tie together surrounding rooms. Inherited Jacobean furniture gains verve with seats reupholstered in ribboned French fabric and cachet of individual pillows in toile de Jouy fabric and piping.

Opposite the fireplace, a graceful teak-and-rattan settee is often pulled into service at the dining-room table to seat large groups. The uncluttered bookshelves make a calm backdrop.

moving walls and
medium-level renovations

THE WRIGHT MOOD

Bob Gregson, an artist and creative director, and Peter Swanson, a physician, couldn't believe their eyes when they came up the driveway. They had just visited Frank Lloyd Wright's 1936 Herbert Jacobs house in Madison, Wisconsin—the prototype for Wright's Usonian houses. They loved the Usonians' elegant, organic simplicity; their open plan; and the way Wright involved nature. In fact, they were looking for property to build a similar home when they found this house, built by a local Connecticut architect in 1956. It had been vacant for two years, receiving "no thank-yous" from hunters of center-hall colonials.

"We immediately saw its potential," says Gregson. "There was no mistaking the Wright inspiration, such as the low roofline, and the fact that the house is so horizontal and grounded that it seems to grow out of the landscape—it's so thoughtfully sited that it seems to disappear and blend into its environment." Like the Jacobs house, this one had strong horizontal lines, full-length glass walls, and a generous interior use of wood; inside, planks of deep-toned redwood had been applied on almost all the walls, and they were in top condition.

The twenty-five-hundred-square-foot four-bedroom became theirs in 1991, and they immediately got to work. The most dramatically visible change was to the exterior, which was originally tan siding with brown trim. The new rich-toned siding was inspired by the Jacobs house.

Inside is architect-designed furniture, art, and sculpture, as well as paintings and pottery from mid-century and

An unimposing moss garden, inspired by a recent trip to Japan, alludes to Wright's Japanese visit in 1913 for the Imperial Hotel project. The dangling sculpture by the front door is by Gregson. A Japanese maple stretches through the carport's opening. The front door's original turquoise was toned down with a pinch of black.

modern artists. Yet instead of looking curated, as so often happens, the home feels inviting because of welcoming placements and a lighthearted approach.

Outdoors, art shows up along the quarter mile of walking paths the owners installed on the perimeter of the two acres. Marking the way are abstract sculptures that Gregson made. Says Gregson, "Every season is great, even winter. When it snows, we turn on the outside lights, sit back, and watch it fall."

Ranch Style SIDING AND COLOR

Previous page: "A companion to the horizon" is how Wright referred to his Usonian houses, which fits the concept of the carport (often credited to Wright): a simpler way than a garage to protect a car, here it also adds breadth to the home.

The exterior is now very much a tribute to the Jacobs house's rich-toned board-and-batten wood treatment. Removed was narrow, painted cedar clapboard. The house was re-sided with 9-inch-wide heartwood cypress joined with 1 1/4-inch-wide redwood.

The foyer's floor-to-ceiling glass walls and corner are another Wright influence. The mid-century Italian lights are presumed to have been made by Dino Martens, an influential Muranese glass designer. The laminated oak table is by Scandinavian Hans Moller for Wor de Klee, 1947. Earthenware is Contempora/Poppy Trail by Metlox, a popular California company in the 1950s.

Wright's concept of nature combined with privacy creates an outdoor dining room that's at once expansive and intimate.

Above: The living room, anchored by a thoroughly redesigned fireplace, is a sophisticated mix of color and form. The fireplace screen was designed by owner Gregson. Eero Saarinen's red Womb chair, 1948, and ottoman relax beside his 1957 Tulip pedestal table. An Isamu Noguchi paper lamp sits on the hearth. From the 1960s, '70s, and '80s, art by Andy Warhol, Sol Lewitt, and Keith Haring adds effervescence.

Opposite: In the 1950s, the sunken living room was not only a way to define space and to encourage the new informality of living-room lounging, it also created visual levels. A theme of circles in the upholstery is echoed on a sanded-plywood plate by Eero Saarinen. On the foyer level, mounted on the wall, is an Eames leg splint.

Ranch Style EERO SAARINEN

An American born in Finland, Eero Saarinen (1910–1961) was one of the preeminent mid-century architects and furniture designers. Two of his most renowned works are the Womb chair and the Tulip series. The 1948 Womb was considered revolutionary for its materials and fluid shape, designed as a new club chair to support contemporary Americans' desire for comfortable lounging, slouching, and curling up. It was made out of molded fiberglass (glass-reinforced plastic) with fabric-covered foam upholstery, on chromium-plated steel legs.

The Tulip series is another architectural approach to furniture. Working with a team of Knoll researchers,

Saarinen wanted to eliminate the clutter of table and chair legs, aiming for each piece to be one continuous piece of plastic, resulting in just one leg. The chair's seat shell was fashioned out of molded fiberglass. But because the material's weight-bearing ability was still unknown, he worked for five years on a suitable base, resulting in an aluminum pedestal that was lacquered to match the seat, creating the look of one material. The dining and side tables used the same base. The strong balance of ample tops on slender stems makes each piece sculptural. Much of Saarinen's most important architectural works were postwar, many of which can be found on campuses such as Yale and MIT.

THE NEW BASICS COOKBOOK
Bobby Flay's **Bold American**
The Encyclopedia of
CREATIVE CUISINE
CLASSIC
HOME COOKIN

Happy-go-lucky 1950s bar stools, re-covered in primary colors, contrast with the neutral wood of the refinished kitchen. "Their backs remind me of old UHF television aerials," says owner Peter Swanson.

Ranch Style KITCHENS

The kitchen was able to breathe once the formerly dark, cramped room was opened up on two sides: one wall was completely removed, while the second was converted into a counter and left free of all upper cabinets. As part of the renovation, more-refined materials were used, replacing the white Formica cabinets and burnt-orange counters. New cabinets were built from rift oak, with redwood trim, to reflect the exterior tones of the house. Sleek white tile makes a stylish backsplash. Complementing the terrazzo floor, the counters were chosen for their stone appearance. Supporting a passion for cooking is a professional stove; underscoring appreciation for the past, the Nutone hood has been retrofitted. Stainless-steel pots hang conveniently at the top of bright floor-to-ceiling windows.

Ranch Style TECHNOLOGY

In 1940, architects Charles Eames and Eero Saarinen won awards in the Museum of Modern Art's competition for "Organic Design in Home Furnishings"—furniture, including casual chairs constructed with molded plywood shells, in fluid shapes. In a breakthrough manner, they had pressed layers of plywood veneers into soft curves. After the war, molded-fiberglass enabled those designs to evolve into a new approach to furniture design, such as Saarinen's famously loungeable 1948 Womb chair and in the Eameses' (Charles and Ray) plastic shell chairs, 1950, made of fiberglass and resin. In 1941, while the Eameses were living in California, the U.S. Navy asked them to develop lightweight, stackable plywood leg splints; postwar, those technologies led to some of the Eameses' greatest furniture.

In the bedroom, the 1930 side table, in chrome with a cork top, is by Gilbert Rohde, known for modern, glamorous furnishings. The black chair, reminiscent of the Eames 1946 molded-plywood chair, and the 1950s lamp were found at Goodwill. The painting is by London-based contemporary architect Zaha Hadid.

VICTORIAN BEACH HOUSE

Carol and Tim Bolton drove right by the same little overgrown patch of road two or three times as the real estate agent zipped them back and forth from one house to another. Finally, Tim yelled for them to stop; he'd seen a flash of pink through the vines. As they pulled onto a side road, the agent chided, "Ya'll are going to hate this place."

Next to a FOR SALE sign was a 1940s pink fisherman's shack constructed from cinderblocks, complete with a bare concrete floor. It had three bedrooms, ideal for a family with two young children, but had been abandoned for years.

Says Carol, "We told her, 'This is it, we love it.' And we made an offer on the spot. Neither of us wanted to play hard to get." Neither did the owner, who accepted.

It's easy to understand why the broker had been showing them more upscale residences. The Boltons own Homestead, a group of six antiques and home-furnishing stores in Fredericksburg, Texas, that has been a pacesetter for country and Texas design, well known for integrating European pieces.

It's also simple to see why they loved the house. While proximity to the water—a block from the Gulf Coast—was a luxury (and why they adopted the name Fineview for their new getaway home), the other attractive feature was that the house needed a lot of work, being close to dilapidated. "That was fine for us, because we wanted to put our own imprint on it, and we knew we could take a moderate budget and create a new house," explains Tim. "We also didn't mind that it was overgrown with vines. We love the seclusion."

They retained the footprint of the house but removed walls, raised ceilings to peak at eleven feet, and gutted the kitchen. Walls were Sheetrocked; windows were replaced and outlined in molding that adds a period quality. Cecilia Berber-Thayer, their friend and a Homestead designer, helped with a theme. "It's a blend of Victorian and fanciful beach house," she says. "And it's very laid-back."

Carol's desire was for the house to feel as if it had been there forever. "I found every photo of any family member at the beach and hung them on the walls. I wanted it to feel as if my grandparents had lived here, too."

Acknowledging that a second home should be a change of scenery and lifestyle, Carol notes, "When we're here, we eat different foods—we live on Gulf shrimp and farmstand potatoes. The only music we listen to is Tony Bennett. We have clothes we wear just here, like big white T-shirts, faded chinos and sneakers, straw hats, and loose gauzy dresses for me. Tim and I save all our magazines, boxes of them, and wait to read them at the coast. We're different people when we're here."

Above: The porch invites relaxing. Green-and-pink metal chairs, with lyrical cutouts, are 1950s American. The unpretentious new porch resembles a deck and blends in with the exterior color. The weathered chairs, nautical lantern, and anchor make the impression of a stylish but unaffected ease of living. Right: In the living room, the feeling is a relaxed step into the 1800s: the coffee table is a tête-à-tête; a fishing net draped over a round table adds texture; lace window panels are casually hung by slipping a piece of wire through a top pocket and wrapping the ends to eyehooks; one long beautiful pillow on the sofa looks like a treasure. The 1800s seascape behind the sofa enhances the palette; hung low, it creates a calm, eye-level horizon.

Previous page: The exterior color, says Carol Bolton, was inspired by "the shiny inside of a seashell." The trim is a soft off-white. Custom molding on the new windows gives them simple, appealing detailing. The rusty sign was found at a Massachusetts flea market.

They've also co-opted a tradition inspired by a friend. "Every day, around five o'clock, we put the kids in the backseat of the car," says Tim, "and we roll down the windows and drive along the beach road. There are two rules: no more than twenty miles an hour, and we have to be gone an hour. We wave at neighbors and stop to talk, and we look at the water. And then we start thinking about what to have for dinner. And that's the pace at Fineview."

Ranch Style KITCHENS

With all the interior kitchen walls removed, as well as several small closets, the room is now open to the dining and living areas. Two-inch-thick oak gives the counters a substantial, furniture effect. New wood cabinets are coated in a mix of metallic gray, blue, and green paint to communicate water. Omitting upper cabinets keeps the feeling open.

The new sofa is slipcovered in textural linen-cotton, with an over-design of ecru damask that seems old-world without being old-fashioned.

A casual mood was achieved through a new open plan. In the dining area, the homey mood is created with vintage French iron chairs painted sage or pink, topped with crocheted tea-cozy shrugs; an antique tablecloth dyed muted green; and chandeliers (their chains softened by pale, silk sleeves) embellished with shells, sea glass, and antique curtain weights.

Ranch Style FLOORING

The owners had planned to work with the old cement floor, but when it would not take a stain (calcium had leached out over time, making it resistant to the process), they decided to try terra-cotta tiles. They glued the tiles—some painted shell pink, others painted gray-green for a border—to the cement, leaving them ungrouted and unsealed to suggest another century.

"The mood is sepia-tone, hand-colored photographs," says designer Cecilia Berber-Thayer. "You can imagine a photo of a woman with pink cheeks and a blue dress—that's the color palette. Then we make it more faded." In the living room, layers of paint in sage and shell pink were rubbed onto the walls.

The master bedroom and an adjoining warren of small closets were gutted. A bath and small dressing area (with new closets) were created on the other side of a wall that stops a few feet short of the ceiling to keep the rooms lofty. The walls project a patina of a bygone era with large-scale fleur-de-lis stenciling.

Old black-and-white family photos are framed, attached to slim chains, and draped like necklaces over an antique sconce. The antique wooden table has the perfect bedside manner.

Ranch Style TEXTURES

A devotion to layers of textures and cream and clay tones evokes unusual elegance in the master bedroom. Linens are a soft stack of antique quilt, chenille throw, and crocheted throw. Pillows and damask-pattern sheets are sewn from vintage fabrics. The teak bed was shipped from India and painted in a green wash. The vintage metal cabinet has earth-tone velvet added to the top and front for depth.

In the guest bedroom, an old wicker chair receives a second life with an added fabric back, set with nail-head trim, and a mix of toile, tea-stained floral, and dotted cording. The iron bed is finished with an antique pillow that spans its width and is encased in gauze. Walls are stenciled in a large damask pattern.

The back of the house is opened by sets of new French doors that replaced sliders, leading onto a new full-length deck. The gothic Adirondack chairs are custom-made. "When I see that row of white chairs," says Carol, "it makes me feel as if I'm on vacation."

HAUTE HIDEAWAY

"It looks like a trailer," says Lee F. Mindel, deadpan, showing a photo of his house's exterior and waiting for a response. A partner at Shelton, Mindel & Associates in Manhattan, he designs some of the most intellectually and internationally acclaimed offices and residences in the world. But this is a modest fourteen-hundred-square-foot weekend house.

Moreover, it's not even part of the glitzy Hamptons beach scene a few miles away; it's in an unassuming community called North Sea—though with a backyard that rolls dockside onto Peconic Bay.

Working with an architect friend, Mindel redesigned the house, doing all the work himself, in only five consecutive three-day weekends focusing on the interior. Because it's a weekend house he wanted ready for summer only two months after he purchased it, the objective was that improvements be quick and inexpensive, and the mood be comfortable and bright.

"It took six coats of white paint," remarks Mindel about the brown walls. Structurally, he took away a wall that closed off the kitchen from the dining room, and he removed another one between two choppy bedrooms to create a large master suite. The rest of the changes were mostly cosmetic.

"I was going for trashy cottage," says Mindel of the interior theme. However, one glance shows a chic mix of beautiful pieces, many of them favorites he has taken with him from house to house over the years, particularly works by the French furniture designer André Dubreuil.

The lack of pretense, and the focus on the most care-free weekend living, can be seen in the rumpled slipcovers and linens and in a straightforward combination of high- and low-cost accessories. In weekend living, time is spent on pleasure.

That pleasure is evident in the contrast of a shy exterior and the surprise of a stylish interior. It's in the fact that a top architect preferred to do the work himself. And it's in all of Mindel's pithy descriptions of his beach house. Such as, "It's fun."

Two small rooms became this large master bedroom, complete with a sitting area. "Taking down a wall made for some hierarchy of space, so that this room has a different dimension from the other bedrooms," owner Lee Mindel explains. Standing on a low birch table from Ikea is a camera-lens candelabra by André Dubreuil, a contemporary furniture and accessory designer known for his metalwork. A large Arts and Crafts mirror creates the illusion of another window.

Ranch Style
WINDOW TREATMENTS

The most inexpensive floor-to-ceiling white curtains that Mindel could find hang in almost every room. "The curtains mask the irregularity of the windows," he says. "And with them, in a house this small, you're not as conscious of how chopped up all the spaces are." Rods are hung all the way across the walls. The final effect adds texture to Sheetrocked walls and softens corners.

Previous page: The 1920 house was no-frills practical, with a protected entrance and front deck added on. Only a whimsical vintage wire lawn chair is a clue that something different is inside.

Ranch Style MANTELS

To give a simple fireplace mantel more presence, a plank of birch plywood was laid across the top, adding a natural tone and acting as another layer of molding. The elegant presentation consists of Sally Gall prints propped alongside a candelabra by Mark Brazier-Jones.

Right: White and sand colors drift through the bedroom, with texture provided by a custom headboard in Ultrasuede and glamour by the curves of a 1950s lamp in lead crystal made by the French Daum family. The low bookcase is by Shelton, Mindel. Below: The living room's blue-and-white theme is at once elegant and contented, filled with pieces Mindel grew up with: the sofa, armchairs, and Bielecky coffee table, and Liberty stools from London.

Ranch Style FLOORING

Wanting one uniform floor throughout the house to conceal various vinyl patterns, Mindel rolled unbound woven seagrass carpet on top of the existing vinyl. Where rooms joined, he cut a floor saddle out of unfinished plybead and nailed it over the seagrass seams. In the kitchen and bath, he repeated the look with vinyl sea grass.

A corner was transformed into a sophisticated foyer, first by installing plywood wainscoting, then by letting the beauty of three unusual curved pieces set the welcome: an André Dubreuil clock; a glass-topped round table; and the airiness of a white wire chair.

Opposite the living-room sofa, two tall, blue glass vases by the famed Murano glass house Vistosi are reminders of the water outside.

Ranch Style WALLS

Mindel turned a bland, windowless wall into an artful space, first by mounting a large mirror to mimic an oversize window. With light coming to the wall, he was then able to introduce beautifully eclectic pieces: the bronzed-steel console, another family piece; the table lamp by Artemide; blue Vistosi vases; and the flying curves of the graceful sconces by André Dubreuil.

Above: Opposite the sink, a thick shelf provides easy, open storage—and an attractive display—of blue-and-white pottery. Silver-tip lightbulbs add a nautical feel and serve as unusual sconces. Right: A lack of fuss on the kitchen walls makes the room seem to double in size. White semigloss paint in the kitchen and throughout the house provides crispness.

Ranch Style KITCHENS

The kitchen was opened up by first removing a wall—but maintaining part of it as a divider—connecting it to the rest of the house. Upper cabinets were completely removed, and plybead was installed to add vertical lines and texture. Lower cabinets were painted inside and out, and one type of new hardware was chosen to unify cabinets and drawers; new appliances continue the flow of white. The counter, in wood-tone Formica, secures the space.

Below: For an unexpected, casual dining table, the owner took a basic wood door and reclined it on two sunshine yellow sawhorses from a home-supply store. French garden chairs, circa 1940, give the experience artful delineation while appearing weightless.

Below right: In a guest room, Power Ranger and Kate bask on a refined slipper chair re-covered in casual blue mattress ticking.

Above: White unites the dining room; pieces inside the breakfront are also white or glass to support the light feeling.

Ranch Style BEDROOMS

To solve the problem of a long, narrow room, the owner did the unexpected: he emphasized it. He positioned a pair of beds foot to foot, allowing a long, large area to be free, making the room seem wider and longer. A small table at the beds' union (rather than lodged against a wall) and a pair of low-scale upholstered chairs add sophistication.

Below: Mindel uses choice pieces of furniture to make up for the lack of architecture in this guest room, with English mahogany beds from the 1860s and a Gothic table and console. An upholstered chair adds refinement, as do the classic accessories. Right: The view from the back of the house at dusk.

GLASS TREE HOUSE

Yanni took one look at the conversation pit, a feature not common to his life in Greece, and immediately exclaimed, "This is it!" His wife, Erin, however, looked around and said, "Well, anything can be changed . . ." They had stepped into a dark 1965 house in Texas that had cramped halls, brown paneling, and a tight kitchen. What Yanni found excitingly American, Erin found astoundingly daunting. The color scheme was classic leftover orange, avocado, and brown. The yard had overgrown in the year it had sat idle. "In fact, there had been an offer to tear the house down," says Erin, "and it had come in higher than ours.

"I think the conversation pit scared away buyers. It was too funky, too cosmic. And you knew the house needed to be changed, but it was hard to see how." Standing in the sunken living room, she peered behind drab curtains, saw the floor-to-ceiling glass walls, and decided that the house had some flair. It also had conveniences such as being set back on a large corner lot, with expanses of yard for their four children, and plenty of room in twenty-eight hundred square feet. "I looked at the deck and side yard, and I could imagine the fun the children would have there."

Ripping down the curtains, the couple marveled at their new living room. "We're up high from the street, with great trees reaching around us. It's like being in a glass tree house." To save money, she and Yanni, an engineering professor, began renovations themselves. "When we got

Previous page: The glass, the angle of the gables, and the assertive horizontal lines call to mind Cliff May's modern houses and elements of Frank Lloyd Wright's 1948 Herman T. Mossberg house in South Bend, Indiana. The owners painted the brick putty green for fresher appeal, etched with black trim.

From the side, the house seems to float. The Japanese influence found in much mid-century architecture is gentle but present, especially in the harmony with the large trees and the way the rock-covered foundation and simple stairs blend into the terrain. The red-orange rail is the only element that seems to separate the house from nature.

stuck, we turned to a book. It's never as hard as you think it is," she says of their experience pitching ceilings and removing walls.

Once the interior was wide open, she designed around inherited pieces, furniture from Greece, and purchases from frequent vacations to Mexico, loading all the children in the car for the drive.

To celebrate, they had their first large party and watched with surprise as the house fully came into its element. "This is a party house," she affirms. "It never feels crowded because the space is so open. People love the novelty of moving from level to level, from the dining room to the living room to the conversation pit. A sixties home is very functional and open, and great fun to live in."

Ranch Style **FOYERS**

To open up the tight entry, the owners removed two walls and raised the ceiling. The Mondrian-inspired custom side-light (replacing a colonial style) introduces the modern feeling of the home, and it sets off the door carved with a different pattern on the interior. Green slate was installed over brick and continues in the kitchen and dining room.

Below left: "It's like having a living room outside," says Erin of the covered deck, with its pale gray overhang. Mexican *equipal* furniture (made of wood and pigskin) helps the space function as a family room. Right: A new, sculptural door, hand-carved in mahogany, was inspired by the work of Lynn Ford, a brother of regional modernist architect O'Neil Ford. The foyer establishes an upbeat, international atmosphere.

Above: The dramatic living room is framed by the long, pitched ceiling, open to air and sky. Right: In the conversation pit, the tin Moroccan tea table fits perfectly. Ample throw pillows and a soft flokati offer comfortable lounging.

Ranch Style FIREPLACES

Wanting a contrast between the conversation pit and the fireplace, the owners used green paint, concealing mismatched bricks in the process. The fireplace screen is Erin's design; she brought a sketch to a welding company who crafted it in iron. To the left, a mahogany cabinet functions as storage and a room divider from the kitchen.

Ranch Style **DOORWAYS**

The owners raised the ceiling in the hallway. Inspired by photos of woven wood doors in a book on Greek style, they had the transom custom-made in a Greek-style basket weave of cypress. "The pattern is functional since it lets air circulate, and it adds an unusual element." They covered the columns with Sheetrock. A checkerboard of small tiles on the risers acts as an energetic play on the transom grid, and as a way to link brick and slate. The sconces are Moroccan.

Left: Textures, colors, and patterns add liveliness to the hallway. Below left: A door from Mexico supplies character to a wall. Below: Transforming a dark bedroom into a dining room, Erin and Yanni removed two walls, raised the ceiling, and installed full-length windows, opening from the top or side. "I'm most proud of this room," Erin admits.

Ranch Style **LOUNGING**

In the 1960s, ranch houses began showing further inventiveness. As the craze for lounging went mainstream, conversation pits provided a cocoonlike, slouch-enabling environment that was slightly separate but still part of the living room. It held the same excitement as another modern innovation—the step-down or sunken living room.

The owner wanted stainless steel for a suggestion of a professional kitchen. "Then I priced it at a kitchen-design store and found that it was out of my range," Erin says. So she faxed the dimensions to a sheet-metal company who quoted one tenth the price and shipped it. "I mounted it over the old Formica backsplash, using Formica glue," she says. "The white cabinets pop against the stainless." Working with the stainless, new Formica counters are speckled with sand, gray, and white.

The concentration in this kitchen renovation is on making the space open and airy, so it feels and performs like a larger room. An opening was cut into a wall of the kitchen, and a set of custom lattice pocket doors was installed to connect the kitchen with the hallway and dining room.

Ranch Style **KITCHENS**

"I like being part of the activities in the house and being able to easily see what the children are up to," says Erin. "So I didn't like that the kitchen was totally shut off. We were determined to find a way to make it part of the living space."

When they pitched the ceiling, they extended it about twelve inches above the interior-wall edge. "This way, the wall would seem to float, as if it were a partition." They planked the ceiling to continue the look of the rest of the house and added a skylight for natural task lighting.

After a wall was taken out, a breakfast bar was added, also serving as a work island. Bar stools, purchased inexpensively from a restaurant-supply house, are covered in Jet Ski fabric. "I wanted glitter and sparkle, something kitschy and spill-proof."

In the rear, a door that leads to a utility space received coats of green, transforming it into more of a screen. "I introduced another color so the kitchen wasn't drenched in white," she explains.

complete renovations
and newly built

PALM BEACH STORY

When the architects finally unwrapped the vintage McDonald's sign, for the owners of this 4,500-square-foot-house it was an ideal fit. It told exactly how far architects Peter Shelton and Lee F. Mindel, partners at Shelton, Mindel & Associates in New York City, had taken the house.

Mindel remembers his first impression, pre-renovation: "It was a typical faux ranch-house hacienda that had no connection to the site." The rooms were showy, with shiny marble travertine floors. The walls zigzagged and turned, and the house was overly full of amenities to promote the impression of opulence

and importance. Ceiling heights were towering and all different. It was, in short, a ranch "McMansion."

The owners had planned to gut the central part of the house, but on a modest budget. Both the clients and the firm wanted to introduce scale and warmth, and to find a way to take in the green views from the golf course behind the house. The architects, with project designer Grace Sierra, hit upon three answers. First was a continuous, sixty-five-foot-long floating ceiling that joins the living room, dining room, and study, disguising their uneven ceilings. Second, they would use sculptural partitions, some of which pivot, to baffle light and to guide perceptions of space and energy. Third, they would address the plethora of different windows, replacing many with new metal storefront systems. Furniture would be a mix of modern—mid-century and contemporary, American and European—for a continuous flow that did not pinpoint one era. "This couple is very open, very smart, and very energetic," says Mindel. "We wanted their home to reflect that."

Previous page: Framed by palm trees, the setting is unmistakably Florida, and the confidently sprawling feeling is clearly ranch. The architects left the front's private, closed feeling and the irregular roofline.

The vintage McDonald's sign, tilted to become abstract, leads in and out of space in a lyrical way. The sofa is by contemporary industrial designer Antonio Citterio, of Meda, Italy.

Ranch Style OPEN PLANS

The living room's ingenious floating ceiling, which houses the lighting system, unifies the public areas and creates a feeling of movement down its sixty-five-foot length. More movement comes from pivoting walls that architect Lee Mindel likens to pinball flippers; closed, the partitions create a guest room. On the right is a floating panel of glass, redefining the concept of walls. "Because the walls don't go fully to the ceiling, you feel the dimension of the whole space," he says.

Ranch Style
AALTO AND BREUER

The works of Charles and Ray Eames and Eero Saarinen were in many ways advancements on fluid designs by Alvar Aalto and Marcel Breuer. At the Finnish exhibit for the 1939 New York World's Fair, Aalto showed the first chair that had ever been made out of one broad, curved piece of plywood for the back and seat; the arms were bent plywood. Hungarian Breuer was a leader in Bauhaus, a machine-driven movement that created furniture out of tubular steel and bent plywood. Some of Breuer's classics are the Wassily chrome-plated tubular steel and leather chair of 1925 and his bent plywood pieces, in anthropomorphic shapes, from the 1930s.

Below: A shelf is cantilevered off the wall, with sandblasted glass recessed into the top. On it are acrylic molds that once contained food and household products. Says Mindel, "They're not dissimilar to the McDonald's sign in their celebration of popular culture." Birch chairs and table are by Scandinavian Alvar Aalto.

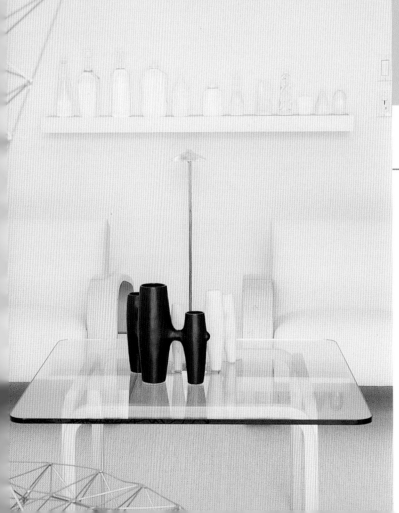

Above: The coffee table, by Tom Dixon, is steel and glass. A long, low bench by the architects is an ode to French designer Charlotte Perriand, who collaborated from 1927 to 1937 with Le Corbusier and Pierre Jeanneret, and with Jean Prouvé in the 1950s. The 1950s pottery was made in California.

Ranch House GEORGE NELSON

The triangular Coconut chair, 1957 (above), along with the 1946 slatted bench and 1956 marshmallow chair, is a George Nelson signature. An architect and writer, Nelson is considered one of the most influential mid-century designers. He took over the furniture manufacturer Herman Miller in 1945, succeeding Gilbert Rohde and bringing in such noteworthy designers as Charles Eames and sculptor Isamu Noguchi, building the Herman Miller image through the 1960s. In his career, Nelson designed houseware, lamps, and home and office furnishings, and clocks for Howard Miller. His series of storage systems reflects a prime concern that was evinced in the 1940s with two storage and cabinet systems, and in the 1950s in his writings on modern living and design.

Above: The primary accent color, yellow, is repeated in the back of the house.

Ranch Style INDOOR-OUTDOOR

The back of the house, completely open, shows the new window system that was installed by enlarging existing openings whenever possible, providing wide and tall vistas from inside and out. The expanse of glass doors turns the house's length into an outdoor gallery—a feature that is taken advantage of with multiple dining and sitting areas that are off every main room.

Left: The dining area is defined by a stationary partition and anchored by a black baby grand. Perfectly matched with the Eero Saarinen table are the Brno chairs, 1930, by Ludwig Mies van der Rohe. The sculptural steel lamp, from 1960s America, is the Boom Lamp, by Jere. Behind the partition is the kitchen.

Ranch Style **KITCHENS**

The kitchen reflects a continuous theme of white, steel, light wood, and glass, replacing a crowded space of dark materials. "The birch plywood floats," says Mindel, also in reference to the floating ceiling. "The one upper cabinet should also seem to hover, distracting the whole concept of upper cabinets." Beside and below the upper cabinet is a sandblasted glass mirror, "like a backsplash that reflects light." The floating ceiling contains strategic task lights, and above there is also cove lighting for diffused light. The lower cabinets, with sliding doors, link the kitchen and family room. On the family-room side, they contain the television and electronics.

The kitchen is calm expanses of birch, glass, and white. Three counter surfaces reinforce the message in birch, glass, and white Corian (solid surfacing). Appliances are stainless steel.

Ranch Style **DRAPERIES**

Floor-to-ceiling linen draperies were used to hide structural columns and to soften the zigzag of some of the walls. Tracks were installed at the extreme top of the walls for maximum impact, and the drapes are hung with direct simplicity, using grommets. The uniformity of the draperies also distracts from uneven windows. In the breakfast room, the curtains hide much of the rough stucco, creating an impression that the walls are entirely glass.

Right: Morning light fills the breakfast room. The expansive, casual effect comes from the low proportions of the pieces: birch table by Alvar Aalto; contemporary wicker-and-wire chairs by Cappellini, Milan. Below: The family room finds a balance of style and comfort, with Jean-Michel Frank club chairs and a 1960s Florence Knoll bench out of tubular chrome. The orange Egg chair and ottoman, by Arne Jacobsen, 1957, resemble an oval interpretation of a wing chair, in molded fiberglass with foam upholstery and a chromed-steel base.

Ranch Style **FLOORS**

When the architects first encountered the house, the travertine floors had been shined to a high gloss, mistaking "more" with luxury. The architects kept the floors but gave them a more interesting and sophisticated finish: the travertine was buffed until it had a matte surface and felt a bit gritty. It became a light platform for the furniture, mimicking the look of sand and providing a more textured surface for the reflection of light.

The master bedroom's impression of being a soft haven comes from layers of white and faint beige textures as varied as terry cloth, canvas, linen, and muslin —and a furry acrylic bedspread that's "part towel, part *Octopussy*." Arne Jacobsen's 1957 Swan chair is covered in canvas. Bedroom floors are wall-to-wall seagrass. On the table, the bubbly 1930s lamps were found in South Beach. The lithograph is a Robert Motherwell, visible through two wire pieces; the white one is a haberdashery display. Alvar Aalto's desk chair is pulled up to a white lacquer Parsons table made by the architects.

MEDITERRANEAN MOMENTS

In back of a red-roofed stone house, a late-afternoon sun beats through the courtyard, the breezes transporting warmed scents of rosemary, oregano, and heady four-o'-clocks. The spill of a fountain mingles with the sound of two dachshunds high-stepping on crunchy gravel in pursuit of an unknown goal. Plates of figs, olives, and stuffed grape leaves are placed on a long limestone table, under a pergola laden with dangling wisteria and vines. This could be Tuscany, Spain, or the south of France. But it's Texas.

The owner of this home, an artist, turned to Sinclair Black & Andrew Vernooy

Architects to dream up the setting. She and Black had been among a group of friends who had driven along the Mediterranean by van for a month, stopping along the way to snap photos of architectural details that caught their eye.

On this rocky acre in a suburb outside Austin, she envisioned a tucked-away home that would look as if a Mediterranean immigrant had settled and built, starting with a small farmhouse and adding onto it over time. "I wanted it a little rough around the edges," she says, "very old-world, as if it could have been in a village. On our trip, I was drawn to rugged, rustic, muscular houses in the south of France that could hold their own in a natural landscape. I wanted this house to look as if it had grown out of great piles of rock that were all around it."

To create a European mood, she asked for a front courtyard set back from a dramatic tier of rounded steps—such as ones she had climbed in Italian villages. The same villages also inspired the wrought-iron arch and gates that frame the distant view of the front doors.

Ideal exposure for every room adds to the village feeling. "Part of Sinclair's brilliance is bringing in breezes and light and siting a house perfectly," she notes. Black placed her home at the top of the wide, sloping lot. Surrounded by typically suburban ranch houses, the house is not visible from the street, tucked behind stands of live oaks. "I wanted the approach to be as untamed and natural as possible, so that you're entering a different time and place," she says.

Black and architectural project manager Greg Thomas designed an H-shaped house, with a center living room and dining room. To make the rest of the living space look as if it were later construction, the architects added one wing of bedrooms and another for the kitchen area, stretching the three thousand square feet into a big footprint that would ultimately shape the grounds.

The limestone throughout is the same material that the owner gravitated to in Mediterranean houses. To dull the glare of freshly quarried white limestone, Black specified a special application whereby mortar was wiped across the façade to add gray tones. Climate considerations are also

Cypress doors, purchased from a local antiques dealer, are painted teal for a Mediterranean cue. Above, a glass canopy shields rain yet invites sun. One bracket is an antique brought back from France, the other is a custom-made copy. Boston ivy stretches across the walls. The rounded stone steps and the height of the fanciful gate and arch set a refined mood.

similar: the sixteen-inch-thick walls serve as year-round insulation, as well as invoke the serious construction of a bygone era. Covered outdoor halls and a courtyard with abundant overhead trellises take the edge off searing sun and add gentility.

With the exotic waft of crushed 'African Blue' basil momentarily hovering in the air, there is a blurring of locale. "While this is more of a Texas house than it is anything else," says the owner, "the inside materials and the wonderful ironwork are because of the skills that European immigrants brought with them."

Previous page: When the house comes into view around a gentle bend, set back from the street, it projects the essence of a home near the Mediterranean Sea.

To give the picnic lawn stronger definition, the grass is bordered in a mosaic of beach stones—black ones from Mexico and blue ones from Indonesia. The owner set them in mortar on edge rather than flat for a stronger relief.

The owner stenciled the wood floors herself, laying the grid on a diagonal to visually increase the space. Once the pine decking was taped out to form the stripes, a greenish gray semitransparent stain was used to fill half the squares, and an oil-based cream glaze for the others. The stenciling continues into the kitchen. The black scroll border is a nod to the exterior gates and awning brackets.

A black Eastlake American breakfront, set against a sixteen-inch-thick wall, establishes the foyer.

An abundance of textures and stone hues give the simple room complexity. The vintage gravel-color marble counters and restrained backsplash were crafted from old bank counters. The surface of the walls was raised by lightly troweling them with a muted cider color. For a clean contrast, linen white was applied to the trim and the exterior of the cabinets, but to echo the ceiling and give the cabinets more depth, interiors are grayish green.

The table, designed by the owner, is a maple butcher-block square onto which three detachable skirts were added; the side facing the sink is skirt-free to allow the table to function as a workstation. "This is my solution to having an eat-in kitchen and a center island in a space that's too tight for both." The pot rack looks graceful in umbrella lines and brings the room into a more personal scale.

A thirteen-foot peak gives the kitchen the feeling of being its own separate building. To impart intimacy, the ceiling is painted a calming robin's-egg blue.

For a narrow window that required privacy from the front courtyard but still needed to pull in light, glass shelves were installed and filled with large glass bottles. Inside the cabinet, linen white shelves are finished with crotchet trim that is tacked on.

In the living room, the eighteen-foot ceiling and open structure suggest a building style from another era, satisfying the owner's wish that this area feel like a barn. Lintels and posts, inside and out, are made from local cedar. The coffee table is cypress.

Ranch Style **FIREPLACES**

The limestone fireplace and arch are from the former 1885 Hancock Opera House. Inside the arch is a trompe-l'oeil painting on plaster of *Boca de la Verita,* an ancient Roman piece depicting a spirit that senses truth. The architects added limestone for width and to dramatically extend the wall all the way to the tall, open ceiling, making the expanse impressively classical.

Ranch Style BEDROOMS

French doors bring the outdoors to the master bedroom. The custom canopy is made out of scalloped, galvanized tin, framed with loose strands of Virginia creeper, grapevines, and wisteria. Inside, the peaked ceiling is painted a blue similar to that of the kitchen and *corredor* but softened with white for a more soothing effect. Drifts of cotton, pale blush curtains are pulled against the posts of a maple bed whose canopy is formed in copper pipes. The painting is by William Hoey.

Below: In the guest room, a large rust-tone tapestry captures full attention, while a framed print, the only other wall hanging, brings focus to eye level. Walls are troweled in a light clay color to add a period element.

Above: The master bedroom opens directly onto the courtyard.

Five sets of French doors that run the length of the living and dining rooms open onto the outdoor hallway.

Above: An alfresco breakfast is set on a Provençal tablecloth, in the company of garden plaques and parakeets.

Ranch Style PORCHES

"Unlike on most ranch houses, there's only one roof overhang on this house, and it's here," says the owner, "expressed as a porch." To soften the slant and to connect the overhang to the sky and courtyard, it is painted multiple coats of bluish green. Sets of French doors create a natural extension of the indoors. Stone walls and floors form a smooth contrast to the knots and bark of ash (juniper cedar) posts.

Above: "I like the look of having many different rooflines," says the owner. The view is toward the *corredor* and into the dining and living areas. Opposite: The architects planned the courtyard to be a suite of rooms; under this pergola is the main dining room.

Ranch Style COURTYARDS

The pergolas are western red cedar arbors resting on juniper cedar posts; the supports are concrete columns that were cast on site. "It was a budgetary decision, since these are one sixth the cost of stone pillars," the owner explains, "but they turned out to be ideal architectural elements. Even though they're modern, the coral color gives them a blurred age and functions as a neutral." Centering the courtyard is a sphere-topped fountain with a base carved from Italian stone. Ringing its stacked-limestone surround are giant orange cosmos, variegated coleus, and copper canyon daisies. The maintenance-free ground cover is gravel. "I like the sound it makes when you walk on it," says the owner. "And it contributes another color element and texture. Instead of adding more green with a lawn, gravel colors warm up the plants."

Ranch Style ENTERTAINING

The outdoor dining room—a ranch house favorite—is given importance by a five-inch-thick limestone table with a length of eleven feet. On it, a late-afternoon repast is laid; to provide contrasting heights, a collection of miniature chairs and tables are used as serving surfaces. "The garden should be a place to enjoy every sense," the owner observes, "fragrance being the most important one." The sensory plan includes abelia, brugmansia, datura, six different roses, spearmint, fig leaves, sweet olive (*Osmanthus fragrans*), nepeta, and jasmine.

HILL COUNTRY HAVEN

In the tradition of the great Lone Star State, Texas is another country. So the passport for Joey and Ed Story should be stamped "England, Thailand, Vietnam, Hong Kong, and finally Texas, all in two and a half weeks." "What I love about being home is, it's Texas—it's absolutely beautiful," says Joey. The trip is not unusual for Ed, an international business executive who is also honorary consul of Mongolia to the United States, and his Kentucky-bred wife, Joey, who writes computer software. Ed worked overseas in Thailand, Japan, and Singapore for many years but always planned to return home. Although the couple also has places in London and Hawaii, at the end of every trip they retreat to one of the highest mesas in the middle of Texas Hill Country, at nineteen hundred feet.

"We knew we didn't want a two-story house because that was all you'd see when you looked up. We wanted a house that blended in with the land," explains Ed.

They commissioned Lake/Flato Architects in San Antonio, a firm recognized for ranch house architecture. Ted Flato and David Lake met when they worked for O'Neil Ford, a renowned architect who reinterpreted frontier and Hispanic structures in a modern way, using indigenous materials and accommodating the climate.

When Ted Flato stood on the mesa with the Storys, Joey already had ideas. "I wanted one giant room to feel like a cabin, and I wanted 'pods'—separate buildings for a lot of the spaces. That way when our three daughters grew up and moved away, we wouldn't have to run air-conditioning in their rooms." Flato and project architect Karla Greer, having pronounced the spot "magical," answered the Storys' dream.

Turning into the ranch, cars kick up clouds on the long, slow caliche road, passing sheep, goats, donkeys, horses, and cattle. Then the road feels as if it's on a nearly 90-degree angle all the way to the mesa. Finally, after a hard turn, the Storys' realization is straight in front of you.

Lake/Flato built the ranch house on a circular plan, with the hub being a thirty-foot-wide, perfectly round reflecting pool. Rough-cut local limestone and galvanized metal make up the five pods that surround it. Except for the living room and dining area (combined into one rectangle), the other structures are bold squares. Geometry shows up again in pyramidal roofs that are a nod to architect Louis Kahn's take on classic forms.

"Having the height to be able to look out and see how the house fits in with everything that's around it makes all the difference," says Ed, dusting his cowboy hat against his jeans. "It's part of where we are. This is home."

Previous page: The structures on the mesa are simple yet commanding, portraying basic protection from the outside world, like circled wagons. To the left is the master wing (the curved wall is part of the master bath); to the right, the study and guest room.

The tall entrance gate, constructed of Douglas fir in a grid pattern, swings open to a walk that runs along the master bedroom, kitchen, and living area. The vine-covered pergola, resting on limestone columns, throws geometric shadows over the court.

Ranch Style STONEWORK

The walls and columns are made out of Old Yella, a local limestone that has a creamy, golden cast rather than white, to handle the glare of the sun and to blend with the ground. The pergola court is paved with "ripple" stone—large, flat pieces of limestone from the level bottom of rivers. The Old Yella limestone is laid in a regional manner called German smear, a construction technique that the immigrants brought with them: the mortar is applied flush with the face of the stones, then it is "sacked" (burlap bags are rubbed over the surface to merge the mortar and stone). "Rather than notice individual stones, you see one solid wall," says project architect Karla Greer.

Ranch Style CEILINGS

In the living room, the owners wanted a refined roof that would be layered in wood like those in Japanese temples. The twenty-foot-high pyramid roof is built from the bottom up: first beams are laid, then the purlins (the horizontal timbers), and finally the decking layer. "Every piece of timber is a supporting piece and true expression of the structure," says architect Flato. "Nothing is for show."

Ranch Style WINDOWS

Large double-hung windows are a Hill Country standard for climate control. In summer, the bottom half is opened to allow breezes to enter the house at sitting level. In colder weather, open tops let in fresh air. The architects made the windows as large as possible for the views as much as the climate.

Made from Douglas fir, the twenty-foot-high pyramid ceiling in the main living area gives the room an exotic, dramatic presence.

In the kitchen, recycled longleaf pine adds warmth to the islands, walls, and cabinetry, while the ceiling is Douglas fir. The counters are local Texas red granite. Far more ingenious than bar stools, these richly textured and hued saddles are supported by tractor tilling disks. In the dining area, the sculptural antler chandelier reinforces the ranch setting, as do the classic Hill Country double-hung windows with fixed transoms. The five-foot-tall standing wine rack was transported from Burgundy.

Ranch Style FLOORS

Floors in the entire master building are concrete. In the living area and master bedroom, it's poured as a three-inch topping slab: on top of a rough slab, a grid of four-foot squares is laid using old recycled longleaf pine. "Each square is poured and hand-worked so that the squares look more like individual tiles," architect Greer explains.

The bedroom reflects the owners' trips to Asia and has the calming feeling of a pagoda. Instilling the mood are a Chinese altar supporting three statues from northern Burma (Myanmar), a silk curtain from Laos, a cabinet from Thailand, and an antique Chinese chair. The bed (originally a coffee table that was lengthened and widened by local craftsmen) is accented with a triangular pillow from Thailand and a blanket from Laos; the one-of-a-kind head-board is a vintage Japanese shop sign made of rice paper and wood. Beside the bed is a red Chinese lacquer table and Thai temple; at the foot, Victorian English stools.

The eclectic room works with the ranch mood of the rest of the house because of the continuity of flooring, the repetition of the tall ceiling and windows, and the open, uncluttered feeling. The stucco walls are hand-troweled to add subtle texture.

The master bedroom has views in two directions: to the contemplative circular pool and, through the three-sided glass bay, to the hills and sky.

One of Lake/Flato's signatures is rooms that stand alone as much as possible. "We can get light, breezes, and views into a room from many more possibilities," says Flato, "than if a room is blocked by another room or a hall. In the Storys' house, views were considered not just from and to a room but *through* a room."

The cupolas provide light to ceilings that, when vaulted, can become dark. With skylights ruled out as an option because of the intensity of the sunlight, a cupola is ideal: it transports diffused light to the interior and shields the room from harsh overhead sun. With two electronically controlled windows that act as vents, each cupola plays a key role in air circulation. "It's the movement of air that makes the difference in feeling cooler," Greer points out. "As air circulates, it's exhausted through open windows in the cupola, forming a natural current."

In the master bathroom, the Asian theme continues, with the sunken tub looking onto a miniature lanai with dwarf bamboo trees; inside the lanai is a Thai Spirit House, where offerings can be made to protect the house. Behind the tub is a collection of Mongolian tobacco pouches and flint sets. The showers are outdoors, with privacy provided by acres of land. "At night, it's spectacular," says Joey. Umbrellas, such as the red one near the shower, are at every door to use when moving from one structure to another during a drizzle.

Ranch Style **O'NEIL FORD**

O'Neil Ford, born in 1905, has been called one of the best unknown architects in America. The charismatic Texan became a leader in regional modernism, opening his own firm in 1934. He was known for translating elements of everyday structures with modern needs, materials, and techniques. High consideration was given to a site's climate, native materials, natural resources, and local craftsmanship; satisfying owners through straightforward inventiveness; providing outdoor living and as much light and air as possible; and building beauty from simplicity and directness. Many of his principles reflect those of Frank Lloyd Wright, whom he admired, and of William Wilson Wurster's ideas of creating a total environment for local conditions. In the late 1930s, he developed his first flat-roof modern house, owing a debt to Richard Neutra. Two of Ford's most famous works are the Trinity University campus in San Antonio and Skidmore College in New York State. Ford was widely known for his generosity to young and beginning architects. He died in 1982.

The study is full-blown western, with collections of Native American and western textiles and artifacts, from vintage horse bits to Navajo silver and weavings. The roundup of rich textures—fur, horn, suede, metal, leather—includes Ed Story's chaps and vintage cowboy hats. Part of the Storys' collection is a vintage children's holster and boots, and an old, well-worn Bible from an early cowboy.

Directly across from the master bedroom are the study and guest room—each one a sixteen-foot square—and connecting bath. Giving each a porch adds a feeling of self-containment. The metal overhangs are reminiscent of old shed designs where shutters can be propped up to give shade and air. The cupolas, lined in Douglas fir, have vents and windows; at night they act as lanterns.

Above: Sheer drama is created by the glass surfaces and reflecting pool; the cupolas light up like steady, self-assured beacons in a solitary compound. Right: A weathered bin finds use as a casual surface for dessert. Opposite: Ed finishes most of his rides by climbing the mesa to this spot. The Storys call this space the front porch because it commands the best views. Westernware adds spirit to the outdoor table.

Ranch Style ROOFS

The galvanized metal roof is called a standing-seam style. Eighteen-inch-wide lengths of metal are laid; where their edges meet, the edges are rolled together; the seam stands 1 1/4 inches tall. "These are lifetime roofs," says Greer of the fireproof material, "lasting fifty to seventy-five years."

TRUE WEST CABIN

On forty-six country acres, this family's life is more packed than when they left a growing Texas suburb. These days, their schedule is shaped by three horses, four dogs, four cats, four birds, and two children.

Debbie and Tony Tilford had talked for years about a dream house. The two-story "McMansions" in the area held no appeal. "We wanted a ranch look of the past, out West, that you could see in Colorado or Nevada," says Tony, who owns his own advertising agency. "A cozy, warm, cabin-in-the-woods feeling. Something comfortable and relaxed and the lifestyle that goes with that. We ended up with something bigger, though, because we have two young teenagers." The 3,700 square feet is divided traditionally, but, in keeping with most new ranch house plans, the master wing is separate from the children's. The cabin feeling is presented in generous expanses of wood, lightened with large windows and views.

The couple also wanted the house to be on the property's cliff to afford dramatic views from every room. "We have the land, and we knew we wanted to build a one-story along the edge so that the house feels part of the terrain rather than as if it were sitting on it," says Debbie.

Tony sketched the house, and architect Chuck Krueger brought it to life. "We had other reasons for a one-story," Tony explains. "I wanted high vaulted ceilings in every room. And we built this to be a house we're going to stay in. Without stairs, we'll have fewer worries as we age."

With the pleasure of a long-term plan, they have established forty-three of their acres as a wildlife preserve for deer, turkeys, owls, songbirds, and other native fauna; the family engages in supplemental feedings, field reseeding, census counts, and habitat control. Bluebird trails are being planned. Father and son are clearing land to plant a putting green out front. Mother and daughter head to the stable and jumping corral to take care of the horses. It's still early morning in this new, energetic vision of family life in an American ranch house.

A true western feeling is established from the start, with rustic-looking materials and textures.

Ranch Style **MATERIALS**

The house definitely announces its western roots. The rambling, asymmetric front is classic ranch, as is the standing-seam galvanized metal roof, here in irregular rooflines that break potential flatness into different planes. The mix of metal and wood is anchored on both ends by stonework. The fieldstone is not flush: "We wanted protruding rocks on the house to create a dimensional look," the owners explain, "and to cast shadows." And rather than set in one direction, the fieldstone is laid on vertical, horizontal, perpendicular, and flat planes to create the energetic crazy-quilt effect found in many of the old local stone houses in the area.

Ranch Style **EXTERIOR**

Fulfilling owner Tony Tilford's idea of a cabin, the house's exterior is pine that has been milled in a style called "bacon strips," maintaining the bark to produce dark, rough-hewn edges. The double-height wall miniaturizes a ten-foot-high entry that is topped with an operable transom for cross-ventilation. Twelve-inch-thick cedar became posts for the broad overhang. The porch is concrete, stained in mahogany and scored on a diagonal grid.

Ranch Style LIVING ROOMS

In the commanding living room, walls are ten feet tall, with ceilings in the main part of the house peaking at eighteen feet. "The trusses are my favorite element of the house," says Tony. The trusses are made of longleaf pine acquired from a demolished 150-year-old cotton mill. "The life rings on the wood show that the trees were 400 years old before they were milled," he says. "A lot of them carry Civil War bullet holes." The fieldstone fireplace wall downplays the height and echoes the exterior's masonry.

Comfortable furnishings mix with a range of textures: a green leather armchair, mauve-and-blue paisley sofas, a soft fringed shawl, and old-fashioned pillows.

Ranch Style LONGLEAF PINE

Recycled longleaf is used for all the wood (except for door and window trim) in the house. Found mostly in northern Florida and southern areas of Louisiana, Mississippi, Alabama, and Georgia, longleaf pine trees were prized for construction and shipbuilding because of their straight and tall growth, tight grain, warm color, and legendary strength and durability. By the end of the nineteenth century the trees were nearly timbered out and unable to reseed. Only longleaf pine recycled from pre-1900 structures is available.

Ranch Style KITCHENS

"We inevitably wind up convening here all day long," Debbie explains, so the room was designed for heavy traffic and lots of separate-but-equal work spaces for salad or sandwich making, newspaper reading, and phone conversations. "Even though it's not modern-looking, it has a commercial feeling," she says. Stainless-steel counters and center-island shelving have a brushed finish to cut down on shine. The center island—a warm extension of the longleaf pine cabinets—conveniently has pots overhead and drawers on both sides. The wrought-iron hardware on the pine doors contributes a period feeling. Adding drama, the open ceiling tops in a triangular window, spilling soft light onto troweled buff-colored walls; an oversize woven basket is placed under the window to add curve.

Opposite: The large, airy kitchen, with its ample island, is the family gathering place.

Above: A professional six-burner, two-oven range with a grill accommodates multiple cooks. Right: An antique table conveys a relaxed mood in the kitchen.

Typical of ranch houses, the back, not the front, is where the house comes alive, invigorated by indoor-outdoor living. Because the wall is lined with large glass windows and doors, the covered porch becomes a natural extension of the living and dining areas.

A side door leads from a garden directly into the kitchen. The limestone for the steps was dug from the terrain.

Ranch Style POOLS

The swimming pool determined the landscaping in the back, leading to a theme of curves that soften the sharp lines of the house. Rounded steps lead from the porch to a curvy dining terrace that follows the outline of the pool, then drops to the sunbathing terrace. The pool is set more than two feet lower than the dining area to create privacy: "When I'm in the water, I can't see the house at all," says Debbie Tilford. "I feel like I'm in a pond."

Set for alfresco dining poolside, the table reflects the family's love for horses; just up from the house are the stable, jumping ring, and corrals.

Rocked by a breeze, a rustic chair swing that's big enough for two transforms the corner into an intimate outdoor room. On the other side of the fencing is part of the wildlife preserve.

Ranch Style **INDOOR-OUTDOOR**

This outdoor living room is as complete as any interior room, with a band of ceiling fans overhead and, underfoot, concrete that has been stained and scored for a polished finish. Comfortable furnishings include a writing desk and a vintage glider: "I love to read out there when it's raining," says Debbie.

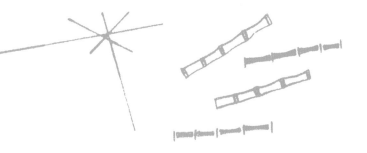

The covered porch has the furnished, generous feeling of an interior room, with its length and naturalness reminiscent of the early *corredors* that were the gathering places in the first ranch houses.

Credits

Produced and styled by Katherine Ann Samon with the exception of A New Riff on Cliff May, pages 73–79, styled by Yolande Yorke-Edgell; Victorian Beach House, pages 125–131, and True West Cabin, pages 179–187, styled by Cecilia Berber-Thayer; Glass Tree House, pages 141–147, styled by Clayton Morgan and the author.

Photography by Edmund Barr with the exception of Haute Hideaway, master-bedroom sitting room (page 134), living-room console (page 136), kitchen/sunflowers (page 137), dining room (page 138), and guest room with two dogs (page 138) by Jonn Coolidge; Palm Beach Story, by Tria Giovan.

For Visuals: Graphic design elements, such as starbursts and boomerangs, from wallpapers and fabrics, by Melinamade Fabrics, 707 Cesar Chavez Street, San Francisco, CA 94124; 415-860-1363; www.melinamade.com. Vintage-style fabrics from Full Swing Textile Collection, 474 Thames Street, Newport, RI 02840; 401-849-9494; www.fullswingonline.com

Resources

A Cook's Paradise

Charles Morris Mount Interior Design, 300 West 108th Street, Suite 2C, New York, NY 10025; 212-864-2937

Architect, Bob Bayley, P.O. Box 399, Ennis, MT 59729; 406-682-4102

Counters, Surell; Cabinetry, Ligna laminate; Formica Corporation, 10155 Reading Road, Cincinnati, OH 45241; 800-367-6422

Glass tiles: Architectural Glass, Inc., 71 Maple Street, Beacon, NY 12508; 845-733-4720

Lighting, Lightolier, 631 Airport Road, Fall River, MA 02720; 800-215-1068

Flooring, kitchen and dining room, Surell, Formica Corporation, 10155 Reading Road, Cincinnati, OH 45241; 800-367-6422

Windows and doors, Andersen Corporation, 1000 Fourth Avenue North, Bayport, MN 55003; 800-426-4261; www.andersenwindows.com

Outdoor light fixtures, Bega, 1000 Bega Way, Carpenteria, CA 93012; 805-684-0533

Secret in the Neighborhood

Mosaics, Celia Berry, 512-453-8307; www.chrisberry@austin.rr.com

Tile, Hacienda Tile, 6335 Camp Bullis Road, San Antonio, TX 78257; 210-698-8479

Dining table, Richard Hicks Home Builders and Furniture Making, 1609 Newning Avenue, Austin, TX 78704; 512-444-7323

Elvis Meets Kuwait

Interior Design, Clayton Morgan, 512-797-6432

Sofa Compact by Charles and Ray Eames, Cappellini Modern Age Furniture Gallery, 102 Wooster Street, New York, NY 10012; 212-966-0669

Italian glassware and pottery, Uncommon Objects, 1512 South Congress, Austin, TX 78704; 512-442-4000

In the outdoor pavilion, chairs and daybed, Ancient Gallery, 920 Congress Avenue, Austin, TX 78701; 512-457-8481

Table, Gardens, 1818 West 35th Street, Austin, TX 78703; 512-451-5492

1850s Romance

Interior design, Courtney & Company, 214 Chester, San Antonio, TX 78209; 210-829-5403; courtco1@aol.com

Builder, James Seiter, Boerne, TX; 210-844-7473

Wall finishes, Hillary Williamson; Courtney & Company

Bamboo bed, from F.O.B., 8507 McCullough, San Antonio, TX 78216; 210-340-5662

Kitchen cabinetry, John Heffel, 3100 FM 2722, New Braunfels, TX 78132; 830-905-3816

Surf Shack Shimmy

Paint, Benjamin Moore, 800-344-0400; walls and ceiling, yellow, HC5; trim and fireplace, off-white, 925; closet door, avocado, HC116; porthole partition, peach, HC53; bedroom wall, grayish blue, 1668

Sunflower painting, by Angelo Bona, Elaine Benson Gallery, 2317 Montauk Highway, Bridgehampton, NY 11932; 631-537-3233

A New Riff on Cliff May

Johnstone Parker Architecture, 16403 South New Hampshire Avenue, Gardena, CA 90247; 310-516-7800

Paint, Dunn Edwards Corporation, 888-337-2468; exterior, Q8-19D; interior, Bone

Plaster work, Trino Gutierrez; 310-266-5928

Dining chairs by Charles and Ray Eames, and bench by George Nelson, from Jules Seltzer and Associates, 8833 Beverly Boulevard, Los Angeles, CA 90048; 310-274-7243

Dining room table and bedroom dresser, from Shelter, 1433 Fifth Street, Santa Monica, CA 90401; 310-451-3536

Fabric, living room chair and bar stools, from Diamond Foam and Fabric, 511 South La Brea Avenue, Los Angeles, CA 90036; 323-931-8148

Kitchen floor, slate, from Dal Tile, 8970 Washington Boulevard, Culver City, CA 90232; 310-559-8680.

Kitchen sink, Elkay 2222 Camden Court, Oak Brook, IL 60523; 630-574-8484

Faucet, Chicago Faucets Company, 2100 South Clearwater Drive, Des Plaines, IL 60018; 847-803-5000; www.chicagofaucets.com

Range, GE Profile, Appliance Park, Louisville, KY 40225; 800-626-2000; www.geappliances.com

Refrigerator, KitchenAid, 2303 Pipestone Road, Benton Harbor, MI 49022; 800-422-1230; www.kitchenaid.com

Bathroom sink, Kohler, 444 Highland Avenue, Kohler, WI 53044; 800-456-4537; www.kohlerco.com

Bathroom light fixture, Halo by Cooper Lighting, 1121 Highway 74 South, Peachtree City, GA 30269; 770-486-4800

Groovy Thing Going On

Harry Bertoia Diamond chairs, kitchen table and chandelier, red vase, The House of Modern Living, 701 Cookman Avenue, Asbury Park, NJ 07712; 732-988-2350

Entry shelf, small red bedside lamp, IKEA, 800-434-4532

Black vase, Fat Chance, 162 North La Brea Avenue, Los Angeles, CA 90036; 323-930-1960

Glass bird, bedroom standing lamp, Twentieth, 8057 Beverly Boulevard, Los Angeles, CA 90048; 323-904-1200

Sofa, Lobel Modern, 207 West 18th Street, New York, NY 10011; 212-242-9075; www.lobelmod@aol.com

Forest silk screen, Mostly Modern, 396 Seventh Avenue, Brooklyn, NY 11215; 718-499-9867

Martini glasses, The American Hotel, Main Street, Sag Harbour, NY 11963

Howard Miller clock, Ethel 20th Century Living, 1091 Queen Street East, Toronto, ON M4M-1K7, Canada; 416-778-6608

Hellerware, A+J 20th Century Designs, 973-378-8102; www.a-j20thcentury.com

Orange chairs, Home Nature, 255 Main Street, Amagansett, NY 11930; 631-267-6647

Bedroom set, Las Venus, 163 Ludlow Street, New York, NY 10002; 212-982-0608

Clear plastic pillows, Target, 800-440-0680; www.target.com

Zen and the Art of Hamptons Living

Landscape, Joseph Cornetta, Joseph Cornetta Designs, 12 Huntington Lane, Water Mill, NY 11976; 631-537-0653

Landscape, Douglas Reed, Reed Hilderbrand Associates, Inc., 741 Mount Auburn Street, Watertown, MA 02472; 617-923-2422

Exterior paint, six ounces evergreen pigment per one gallon of Cordovan Brown OVD Cabot stain; Interior paint, China White, Benjamin Moore, 800-344-0400,

Japanese lantern, dining room, Miyamoto, 75 Washington Street, Sag Harbour, NY 11963; 631-725-1533

Floors in dining room and living room, DutchBoy, deck paint, 2P20, 800-642-8468

Coffee table, Aero, 132 Spring Street, New York, NY 10012; 212-966-1500

Bathroom cabinet and bedroom bureaus, Hunters and Collectors, P.O. Box 1932, Bridgehampton, New York 11932; 631-537-7066

Fifties Cool

Paint, Pratt & Lambert, 800-289-7728; front porch and door, Shaded Spruce 1481-3; exterior trim, Pine Tree Pin, 1419-3; living room, Chelsea Prize 1014, and Golden Tan 2089, acrylic, flat finish

French Cottage

Landscape, Joseph Cornetta, Joseph Cornetta Designs, 12 Huntington Lane, Water Mill, NY 11976; 631-537-0653

Landscaping for the bed with the espaliered apple tree, Charles E. Marder, Marders, Snake Hollow Road, Bridgehampton, NY 11932; 631-537-3700

Espaliered pear trees, Nabel's, 1485 Mamaroneck Avenue, White Plains, NY 10605; 914-949-3963

M. Castellan Landscaping, 411 Ward Avenue, Mamaroneck, NY 10543; 914-381-1399

Contractor, Esteban Garcia, ICO's Paint and Home Improvement, 167 Pelham Road, New Rochelle, NY 10805; 914-576-0608

Terrace stone work, Bruce Heutchy, P.O. Box 312, Larchmont, NY 10538; 914-698-2309

Paint, Benjamin Moore, 800-344-0400; exterior, Navajo White; exterior trim, white; front door exterior, Richmond Bisque; foyer, 952; sitting room, 487; dining room, 1510

Front door millwork, Stripling Black Lumber Company, 3400 Steck Avenue, Austin, TX 78766; 512-465-4200

Front door architectural hardware, Architects & Heroes, 1809 West Thirty-fifth Street, Austin, TX 78703; 512-467-9393

Wallpapers and pillows, Pierre Deux Fabrics, 870 Madison Avenue, New York, NY 10021; 212-570-9343

Foyer ceiling dome, Focal Point Architectural Products, Inc., P.O. Box 93327, Atlanta, GA 30377; 800-662-5550

Rugs, Carpet Trends, 5 Smith Street, Rye, NY 10580; 914-967-5188

Lighting, foyer chandelier, by David Landis; sitting room ceiling light, by Leucos; at Lightforms, 509 Amsterdam Avenue, New York, NY 10024; 212-875-0407

Straw and leather bags, Furla, 727 Madison Avenue, New York, NY 10021; 212-755-8986

Bamboo Roman shade, Smith + Noble, P.O. Box 1838, Corona, CA 92881; 800-248-8888; www.smithandnoble.com

Photography, Thom Harrigan, 617-524-9176

Kitchen faucet, Chicago Faucets Company, 2100 South Clearwater Drive, Des Plaines, IL 60018; 847-803-5000; www.chicagofaucets.com

Black-and-white toile fabric and shade kit, Calico Corner, 800-213-6366

Cabinet knobs, Klaff's, 28 Washington Street, South Norwalk, CT 06854; 203-866-1603

Drawer pulls, Restoration Hardware, 800-762-1005; www.restorationhardware.com

The Wright Mood

Kitchen counters, Fountainhead solid surfacing, Formica Corporation, 10155 Reading Road, Cincinnati, OH 45241; 800-367-6422

Thermador, 5551 McFadden Avenue, Huntington Beach, CA, 92649; 800-735-4328; www.thermador.com

Wolf, 2866 Buds Drive, Fitchburg, WI 53719; 800-222-7820; www.wolfappliance.com

Victorian Beach House

Homestead, 230 East Main, Fredericksburg, TX 78624; 830-997-5551; www.homesteadstores.com

Interior design, Cecilia Berber-Thayer, Homestead, 230 East Main, Fredericksburg, TX 78624; 830-990-0336

Wall finishes, Thomas J. Proch, 508 Cora, Fredericksburg, TX 78624; 830-997-6919

Haute Hideaway

Shelton, Mindel & Associates, 216 West 18th Street, New York, NY 10011; 212-243-3939; smaconnect@aol.com

Glass Tree House

Front door, by Brooks Wright, Boston, MA; 617-327-7857

Front door sidelight by Kathleen Ash, Studio K Glassworks, 2311 Thorton Road, Suite K, Austin, TX 78704; 512-443-1611; www.studiokglass.com

Coffee table, David Marsh, at Eclectic Furniture and Folk Art, 700 North Lamar, Austin, TX 78703; 512-477-1816

Outdoor tablecloth, Cornerstone, 3801 Bee Caves Road, Austin, TX 78746; 512-327-0404

Randolph Howard, 512-327-6257; www.randolphhowardartist.com

Pittsburgh Paint, 407-293-2206, Casino Green kitchen door, 7424

Palm Beach Story

Architecture and interior design, Shelton, Mindel & Associates, 216 West 18th Street, New York, NY 10011; 212-243-3939; smaconnect@aol.com

Breakfast area chairs, Cappellini Modern Age Furniture Gallery, 102 Wooster Street, New York, NY 10012; 212-966-0669

Mediterranean Moments

Architects, Sinclair Black & Andrew Vernooy, AIA, 208 West 4th Street, Suite 3A, Austin, TX 78701; 512-474-1632; www.blackvernooy.com

Builder, David L. Dalgleish, Dalgleish Construction Company, 4019 Spicewood Springs Road, Austin, TX 78759; 512-346-8554

Paint Colors, Kelly-Moore Paint Co., 800-772-7408; front doors, V 38-2 Milford Blue; covered porch ceiling, S 32-2 Teal Plume; teal garden doors, T 18-2 Knight's Landing; dining room walls, G 13-2 Western Sunset flat latex with two sponged-on applications of thin water-based sienna-color glaze; kitchen ceiling, S 31-1 Bird's Egg semi-gloss enamel; kitchen walls, G 28-2 Spiced Cider flat latex; kitchen trim and cabinets, OW21 Linen White semi-gloss enamel; kitchen cabinet interiors, S 17-2 Olivia, semi-gloss enamel; master bedroom ceiling: one part S 31-1 Bird's Egg semi-glass enamel, one part white

Iron work for front gates, awning brackets, kitchen pot hanger, by Adele Riffe Custom Metal Work, 1511 Eva Street, Austin, TX 78704; 512-444-3387

Fireplace trompe l'oeil painting in arch, Jorge Alberto Gonzalez, 410-235-9969; http://jag4art.tripod.com

Butcher-block table and skirt by Mark Landers, Mark Landers' Studio, 404-B Baylor Street, Austin, TX 78703; 512-472-9663

Courtyard fountain, by James David and Bill Bauer at Gardens, 1818 West 35th Street, Austin, TX 78703; 512-451-5492

Garden doors, Brad Crider, 6 Sugar Creek, Austin, TX 78746; 512-327-7083

Master bedroom painting by William Hoey, Gallery at Shoal Creek, 1500 West 34th Street, Austin, TX 78703; 512-454-6671; www.gshoalcreek.com

Hill Country Haven

Architects, Lake/Flato Architects, Inc., 311 Third Street, San Antonio, TX 78205; 210-227-3335

Antiques, The Comfort Common, 717 High Street, Comfort, TX 78013; 830-995-3030; www.comfortcommon.com

True West Cabin

Architect, Chuck Krueger Architect, 5524 Bee Caves Road, Suite G1, Austin, TX 78746; 512-327-5306

Builder, Michael Thames, 1900 FM 967, Buda, TX 78610; 512-312-1717

Antiques and accessories, Homestead, 230 East Main, Fredericksburg, TX 78624; 830-997-5551

Additional resources

1950, 440 Lafayette Street, New York, NY 10003; 212-995-1950

280 Modern, 280 Lafayette Street, New York, NY 10012; 212-941-5825

Art and Industrial Design, 399 Lafayette Street, New York, NY 10003; 212-477-0116

City Barn Antiques, 269 Lafayette Street, New York, NY 10012; 212-941-5757

Elan, 345 Lafayette Street, New York, NY 10012; 212-529-2724

Guéridon, 359 Lafayette Street, New York, 10012; 212-677-7740

Herman Miller, 2855 44th Street, Grandville, MI 49418; 800-646-4400; www.hermanmiller.com

Heywood-Wakefield Company, 2300 S.W. 23rd Street, Miami, FL 33145; 305-858-4240; www.heywood-wakefield.com

Isamu Noguchi Foundation, 32-37 Vernon Boulevard, Long Island City, NY 11106; 718-721-2308

Knoll, 1235 Water Street, East Greenville, PA 18041; 800-343-5665; www.knoll.com

Lost City Arts, 18 Cooper Square, New York, NY 10003; 212-375-0500

MoMA Design Store, 44 West 53rd Street, New York, NY 10019; 800-447-6662; www.momastore.org

Tri-State Antiques, 47 West Pike Street, Canonsburg, PA 15317; 724-745-9116; www.tri-stateantiques.com

Recommended Reading

Albrecht, Donald. World War II and the American Dream. London, England, and Cambridge, Mass.: National Building Museum and MIT Press, 1995.

Albrecht, Donald, et al. The Works of Charles and Ray Eames: A Legacy of Invention. New York: Harry N. Abrams, 1997.

Baker, John Milnes. American House Styles: A Concise Guide. New York: W. W. Norton & Company, 1994.

Clark, Clifford Edward, Jr. The American Family Home, 1800–1960. Chapel Hill, N.C.: University of North Carolina Press, 1986.

Clausen, Meredith L. Pietro Belluschi. Cambridge, Mass.: MIT Press, 1994.

Cygelman, Adèle. Palm Springs Modern. New York: Rizzoli International, 1999.

Dietsch, Deborah K. Classic Modern: Midcentury Modern at Home. New York: Simon & Schuster, 2000.

Garvin, Alexander. The American City: What Works, What Doesn't. New York: McGraw-Hill, 1995.

Garvin, Alexander. Parks, Recreation, and Open Space: a Twenty-First Century Agenda. Chicago: Planners Press, 2001.

George, Mary Carolyn Hollers. O'Neil Ford, Architect. College Station, Tex.: Texas A&M University Press, 1992.

Germany, Lisa. Harwell Hamilton Harris. Austin: University of Texas Press, 1991.

Greenberg, Cara. Mid-Century Modern. New York: Harmony Books, 1984.

Hiesinger, Kathryn B., and George H. Marcus. Landmarks of Twentieth-Century Design. New York: Abbeville Press, 1993.

Hille, R. Thomas. Inside the Large Small House: The Residential Design Legacy of William W. Wurster. New York: Princeton Architectural Press, 1994.

Lake/Flato. Gloucester, Mass.: Rockport Publishers, Inc., 1996.

May, Cliff, and Sunset Magazine. Western Ranch Houses. Santa Monica, Calif.: Hennessey & Ingalls, 1999; reprint of 1946 edition published by Lane Publishing Company.

May, Cliff, and Sunset Magazine. Western Ranch Houses by Cliff May. Santa Monica, Calif.: Hennessey & Ingalls, 1997; reprint of 1958 edition published by Lane Publishing Company.

McAlester, Virginia, and Lee McAlester. A Field Guide to American Houses. New York: Alfred A. Knopf, Inc., 1984.

McCoy, Esther. Case Study Houses 1945–1962. Santa Monica, Calif.: Hennessey & Ingalls, 1962.

National Parks Service. Guidelines for Evaluating and Documenting Historical Residential Suburbs for Listing in National Register of Historic Places. Washington, D.C.: U.S. Government Printing Office, 2002.

Pfeiffer, Bruce Brooks, and David Larkin. Frank Lloyd Wright: The Masterworks. New York: Rizzoli International Publications, Inc., 1993.

Treib, Marc. An Everyday Modernism: The Houses of William Wurster. San Francisco and Berkeley and Los Angeles, Calif.: San Francisco Museum of Modern Art and University of California Press, 1995.

Venable, Charles L. China and Glass in America, 1880–1980: From Tabletop to TV Tray. Dallas and New York: Dallas Museum of Art and Harry N. Abrams, Inc., 2000.

Winter, Robert. Toward a Simpler Way of Life. Berkeley, Calif.: University of California Press, 1997.

Acknowledgments

I owe great thanks to the many scholars mentioned within this book who were magnanimous with their time and knowledge.

Many thanks to my editor, Chris Pavone, for his thoughtful and sophisticated guidance, to Pam Krauss for believing in the project and bringing me on board, and to Jan Derevjanik for this beautiful design. I am also grateful to my agent, Alice Martell, for her support and invaluable advice.

Sincere appreciation to Margaret Russell, Ellen O'Neill, Laura Hull, and Fredrika Stjarne for their smart and generous input.

Kathryn Keller was available with her intelligent advice every step of the way. Colleagues to whom I also owe a debt of thanks for their support are Charlotte Barnard, Cathy Cavender, Mary Ann Howkins, Michelle Stacey, and Leslie Tung. Edmund Barr deserves thanks for these beautiful photos, as does Suzanne Sickner for helping so superbly from California. Many thanks as well to Marysarah Quinn, Mark McCauslin, Joan Denman, Nancy Stabile, and Ronnie Grinberg, at Clarkson Potter. The largeheartedness of Tara Newman and Ted Conklin requires special note. To Jonn Coolidge, Warner Walcott, and Elaine and Paul Rocheleau, I very much appreciate your help, talent, and generosity. I am also grateful for the talent of Cecilia Berber-Thayer, Yolande Yorke-Edgell, and Clayton Morgan, as well as Melina Copass, Michele Mancini, and Katie Roan. Lending their help behind the scenes were Bill Anderson, Kenise Barnes, Susan Pulterman, Alec and Amanda Beck, Sharon and Sean Epps, Kati Korpijaakko, Ann and Jeff Morris, Charles Rose, Michael W. Stanton, and Debbie and Tony Tilford.

Loving thanks to my husband, Larry; son, David; and brother George, for their support and for living with this project for several years. I am very grateful to the homeowners featured in these pages, for their generosity in opening their homes to me as well as for their continuous contributions to the book. Like their houses, they are a special group. And great thanks to the creative minds that conceived the early ranch houses with their indomitable spirit, intelligence, and love for America.

Index